הִנֵּנִי

PRAYERBOOK HEBREW
FOR ADULTS

Rabbi Nina Beth Cardin

Activities:

Lori Lyons

Terry S. Kaye

Editorial Consultants:

Rabbi Ken Chasen

Rabbi Joel Soffin

Behrman House, Inc.
www.behrmanhouse.com

Book and Cover Design: Joe Buchwald Gelles
Art by Ilene Winn-Lederer; Clare Sieffert 28, 99
Project Editor: Terry S. Kaye

The publisher gratefully acknowledges the cooperation
of the following sources of photographs for this book:

Shirley Berger 67; Creative Image Photography cover, 13, 16, 29, 41, 42, 47, 105, 107;
Gila Gevirtz 5, 45, 63, 96; John T. Hopf 35; Terry Kaye 60, 77, 117, 127;
Richard Lobell 11, 15, 23, 109, 130, 133; Ginny Twersky 34, 98, 123; Vicki Weber 79

Cover photograph:
Congregation Agudath Israel, Caldwell, New Jersey

Table of Contents

בְּרָכוֹת 1

Blessings abound in the Jewish imagination, binding themselves to the Jewish spirit, weaving themselves in and out of the hours of the day. There are blessings that speak of joy and blessings that speak of sadness, blessings that seek answers and blessings that offer thanks, blessings that recall the past and blessings that point toward the future. But all these blessings have one thing in common. They seek to answer one of life's basic questions: What really matters?

Blessings are life's highway markers, spiritual touchstones that announce: Pay attention to this. They focus us on things that we might otherwise overlook. They help us plot a noble destination, guiding us in that direction. And when they are most successful, they open in us feelings of appreciation, purpose, and sacred awareness.

Most blessings begin with these six words:

בָּרוּךְ אַתָּה, יְיָ אֱלֹהֵינוּ, מֶלֶךְ הָעוֹלָם . . .

Blessed are You, Adonai our God, Sovereign of the universe . . .

Can you recall a time when you said a blessing?
What was the occasion?

In your opinion, did saying a blessing heighten or change the moment?
If so, how?

_____

_____

_____

_____

PRAYER DICTIONARY

בָּרוּךְ
blessed, praised

אַתָּה
you *(He max angular)*

יְיָ
Adonai

אֱלֹהֵינוּ
our God

מֶלֶךְ *KING*
sovereign

הָעוֹלָם
the world

BUILDING YOUR VOCABULARY

Let's begin building a prayer vocabulary with the six opening words in most בְּרָכוֹת ("blessings"). Circle the Hebrew word that corresponds to the English.

Adonai	שֵׁם *Name*	(יְיָ) *he*	אַתָּה
sovereign	(מֶלֶךְ)	כְּבוֹד *HOLY*	יִשְׂרָאֵל *Israel*
the world	נֶאְדָּר	(הָעוֹלָם)	כָּמֹכָה
our God	בָּאֵלִם	מַלְכוּתוֹ	(אֱלֹהֵינוּ)
blessed, praised	שְׁמַע	בַּקֹּדֶשׁ	(בָּרוּךְ)
you	(אַתָּה) *HE*	מִי *WHO*	אֶחָד

FIND THE WORDS

The blessing opening contains four words that refer to God.

Underline these words on the previous page and read them aloud.

There are blessings we can recite on encountering the grandeur of nature.

Beginnings and Endings

Read the following four בְּרָכוֹת aloud and, in each case, underline the six words that usually begin a בְּרָכָה.

You will notice that the ending of each בְּרָכָה changes to reflect the experience that we wish to sanctify. Circle the words that conclude each בְּרָכָה.

Are you surprised that there is a בְּרָכָה to recite upon hearing thunder? Why or why not?

On Eating Bread

בָּרוּךְ אַתָּה, יְיָ אֱלֹהֵינוּ,
מֶלֶךְ הָעוֹלָם,
הַמּוֹצִיא לֶחֶם מִן הָאָרֶץ.

Blessed are You, Adonai our God,
Sovereign of the universe,
who brings forth bread from the earth.

On Drinking Wine or Grape Juice

בָּרוּךְ אַתָּה, יְיָ אֱלֹהֵינוּ,
מֶלֶךְ הָעוֹלָם,
בּוֹרֵא פְּרִי הַגָּפֶן.

Blessed are You, Adonai our God,
Sovereign of the universe,
who creates the fruit of the vine.

On Seeing Lightning

בָּרוּךְ אַתָּה, יְיָ אֱלֹהֵינוּ,
מֶלֶךְ הָעוֹלָם,
עֹשֶׂה מַעֲשֵׂה בְרֵאשִׁית.

Blessed are You, Adonai our God,
Sovereign of the universe,
who continues the work of creation.

On Hearing Thunder

בָּרוּךְ אַתָּה, יְיָ אֱלֹהֵינוּ,
מֶלֶךְ הָעוֹלָם,
שֶׁכֹּחוֹ וּגְבוּרָתוֹ
מָלֵא עוֹלָם.

Blessed are You, Adonai our God,
Sovereign of the universe,
whose power and glory
fill the world.

Did You Know?

Saying אָמֵן after someone else has recited a blessing is an expression of agreement, promise, and encouragement. It says to the one praying, "We are with you," "Let it be so," or "You got that right!" אָמֵן said with full intent is equivalent to having said the blessing yourself. אָמֵן is related to the words that mean "truth," "faith," "trust," and "confidence." Declaring אָמֵן is an act of solidarity that gives the prayer a final push as it makes its ascent from the heart.

בָּרוּךְ

Shoresh

"blessed"

Hebrew words are built on a system of roots. A root — שׁוֹרֶשׁ — consists of three letters from which related nouns, verbs, and adjectives are formed.

Words built on the root ברכ have "bless" as part of their meaning. The following four words share the root ברכ. Circle the root letters in each word.

לְבָרֵךְ בְּרָכָה בָּרוּךְ בְּרָכוֹת

(Note: כ changes to ך when it is the final letter of a word.)

בָּרוּךְ ("blessed") is a passive form of the root ברכ, which, when it forms a noun, means "knee." בָּרוּךְ indicates the one who is bowed to (by bending the knee). Blessing is a gift of admiration and respect that elevates both giver and receiver.

אַתָּה

"you"

The opening words of a blessing put us face-to-face with God. Depending on our intent, we may come boldly, or intimately, or devotedly before God to state our purpose: to praise or plead or thank or even challenge. And yet somewhere in the midst of this encounter, we retreat a bit, turning our second-person audience (אַתָּה — "You") into a third-person reference (מֶלֶךְ — "Sovereign").

Read the beginning of the blessing formula aloud and notice where the shift happens from referencing God in the second person to the third person.

מֶלֶךְ

"sovereign"

מֶלֶךְ הָעוֹלָם is a name given only to God.

This phrasing is an example of *s'michut*, a Hebrew grammatical form indicating the possessive ("of"), in which two nouns combine to create a new term. In this case מֶלֶךְ ("sovereign") and הָעוֹלָם ("the world" or "the universe") combine to form a name for God. Another example of *s'michut* appears in the blessing over wine or grape juice — פְּרִי הַגֶּפֶן ("the fruit of the vine"). Here, "fruit of the vine" forms a new term that refers specifically to grapes. *NAGAFEN PORE*

Similarly we say חֲנֻכַּת הַבַּיִת ("the dedication of the house") when we put up a mezuzah, and at Purim we read from מְגִלַּת אֶסְתֵּר ("the scroll of Esther").

מֶלֶךְ literally means "sovereign" or "king," in this case one who is benevolent as well as powerful.

מֶלֶךְ is built on the root מלכ ("rule"). The following four words share the root מלכ. Circle the root letters in each word.

מַלְכוּתְךָ הַמְּלָכִים מַלְכֵי מֶלֶךְ

הָעוֹלָם

"the universe," "the world"

הָעוֹלָם is the world, the entire universe — in fact, everything. The blessing suggests that there is nothing that is beyond God's realm or outside God's domain. God is not sometimes. God is not here but not there. God is always and God is everywhere.

Circle the prefix הַ or הָ ("the") in each word below.

הָעֵץ הָאָרֶץ הַגֶּפֶן הָעוֹלָם

בִּרְכַּת הַמָּזוֹן

When a meal begins with bread, it ends with thanks after the meal, too — בִּרְכַּת הַמָּזוֹן. This cluster of four blessings traces its origins back to the earliest years of rabbinic Judaism (first century CE). Like most blessings, this one, too, uses the plural form — "us" or "our." No matter whether we eat alone or with hundreds of others, we say "us," reminding ourselves of our shared humanity, our common needs, and our mutual responsibility.

The first paragraph reminds us that God has outfitted the world with all the goodness it needs to sustain us. It is up to us to become partners with God and the land, to create a sustainable environment and a just economy, so that no one will ever go hungry.

PRACTICE:

Read this section of בִּרְכַּת הַמָּזוֹן.

בָּרוּךְ אַתָּה, יְיָ אֱלֹהֵינוּ,	Blessed are You, Adonai our God,
מֶלֶךְ הָעוֹלָם,	Sovereign of the universe,
הַזָּן אֶת הָעוֹלָם	Who provides sustenance
כֻּלוֹ בְּטוּבוֹ,	to all the world with goodness,
בְּחֵן בְּחֶסֶד וּבְרַחֲמִים.	with grace, with loving-kindness, and with compassion.
הוּא נוֹתֵן לֶחֶם לְכָל בָּשָׂר,	God provides food for all living things,
כִּי לְעוֹלָם חַסְדּוֹ.	for God's loving-kindness is all-encompassing.
וּבְטוּבוֹ הַגָּדוֹל	Out of God's great goodness
תָּמִיד לֹא חָסַר לָנוּ,	God has never caused us to lack
וְאַל יֶחְסַר לָנוּ מָזוֹן לְעוֹלָם וָעֶד.	and God will never deprive us of sustenance.
בַּעֲבוּר שְׁמוֹ הַגָּדוֹל,	(All of this) is on account of God's great name,
כִּי הוּא אֵל זָן וּמְפַרְנֵס לַכֹּל,	and God sustains and provides for everything,
וּמֵטִיב לַכֹּל, וּמֵכִין מָזוֹן	and gives adequately to everything, and prepares sustenance
לְכָל בְּרִיּוֹתָיו אֲשֶׁר בָּרָא.	for all the creatures that God has created.
בָּרוּךְ אַתָּה יְיָ,	Blessed are You, Adonai,
הַזָּן אֶת הַכֹּל.	who provides sustenance for everything.

The term בִּרְכַּת הַמָּזוֹן is another example of *s'michut*, the Hebrew construct indicating the possessive form. Literally, the words mean "the blessing of the food" or "the blessing over the food." Together, the words combine to form the name for Grace after Meals.

Why do you think Judaism finds the moments before and after a meal to be opportunities for blessings?

בְּרָכוֹת שֶׁל מִצְוָה 2

Rituals that the Torah commands to us, such as eating matzah on Passover or circumcising a son, are preceded by a בְּרָכָה that speaks of the covenantal nature of the deed. Such a בְּרָכָה is known as a בְּרָכָה שֶׁל מִצְוָה ("blessing of commandment" or "blessing of mitzvah"). In this way, the blessing marks the ritual as an intentional, and joyful, fulfillment of the commandment. For it is in part through the self-conscious performance of these deeds that we bring a spark of holiness into our lives.

Blessings of mitzvah always begin with the same ten words:

בָּרוּךְ אַתָּה, יְיָ אֱלֹהֵינוּ,	Blessed are You, Adonai our God,
מֶלֶךְ הָעוֹלָם,	Sovereign of the universe,
אֲשֶׁר קִדְּשָׁנוּ	who makes us holy
בְּמִצְוֹתָיו	through God's commandments
וְצִוָּנוּ . . .	and commands us . . .

An Ethical Echo

Why is the word "mitzvah" sometimes translated as "commandment" and sometimes as "good deed"?

Perhaps because there are two types of mitzvot: *ritual mitzvot*, which have to do with our relationship with God (such as lighting Shabbat candles and keeping kosher), and *ethical mitzvot*, which have to do with our relationship with one another (such as visiting the sick and giving tzedakah). Both types of mitzvot imply a sense of duty. But ethical mitzvot can rise beyond duty to acts of kindness for their own sake. It is through such acts of helping people who cannot help us back, being moved by suffering half a world away, aiding people we have never even met, that true, unconditional goodness is released into the world.

PRAYER DICTIONARY

אֲשֶׁר
who

קִדְּשָׁנוּ
makes us holy

בְּמִצְוֹתָיו
with God's commandments

וְצִוָּנוּ
and commands us

BUILDING YOUR VOCABULARY

Underline the four words that identify a בְּרָכָה שֶׁל מִצְוָה in the line below.

בָּרוּךְ אַתָּה, יְיָ אֱלֹהֵינוּ, מֶלֶךְ הָעוֹלָם,

אֲשֶׁר קִדְּשָׁנוּ בְּמִצְוֹתָיו וְצִוָּנוּ . . .

At the Root

Words built on the root קדש have "holy" as part of their meaning. The following four words share the root קדש. Circle the root letters in each word.

קָדוֹשׁ   קִדְּשָׁנוּ   קְדוּשָׁה   קָדוֹשׁ

Time and again in the Torah, a commandment ends with the words: "Be holy, for I, Adonai your God, am holy." Action leads to holiness. As God "clothes the naked," so can we. As God "comforts the mourners," so can we. As God "performs deeds of loving-kindness," so can we.

Saying a blessing before eating matzah marks the ritual as an intentional, and joyful, fulfillment of the commandment in the Torah.

Prayer Building Blocks

קִדְּשָׁנוּ

"makes us holy"

קִדְּשָׁנוּ is made up of two parts:

קִדֵּשׁ means "makes holy."

נוּ means "us" or "our."

Judaism teaches that it is important to be part of a קְהִילָה קְדוֹשָׁה, a holy community. Jewish prayer is a shared experience. While we can pray anywhere, any time, we are bidden to pray in a community. Some prayers are recited in a minyan (a gathering of ten adults). Most prayers, even when said alone by an individual, are written in the plural: Our God, We thank you, Heal us. When we turn to prayer, wherever we are, we are not alone.

בְּמִצְוֹתָיו

"with God's commandments"

בְּמִצְוֹתָיו is made up of three parts:

בְּ at the beginning of a word means "with" or "in."

מִצְוֹת means "commandments."

יו at the end of a word means "his" or "God's."

וְצִוָּנוּ

"and commands us"

וְצִוָּנוּ is made up of three parts:

וְ at the beginning of a word means "and."

צִוָּ means "commands."

נוּ means "us."

The letter combination צַו appears in the words below. These letters help us recognize that "command" is part of the words' meanings.

Circle צ and ו in each word.   מִצְוָה   וְצִוָּנוּ   בְּמִצְוֹתָיו

LOOK ALIKES

Sometimes the letter *vav* looks like the vowel sound "oh": וֹ

However, וֹ has the sound "vo" if it follows a letter that already has a vowel, as in עֲוֹ and צְוֹ.

Read each sound aloud.

עֲוֹ   צְוֹ   עוֹ   עֲוֹ

צְוֹ   עוֹ   צוֹ   צְוֹ

Practice reading the following words.

1.	מִצְוֹת	רָצָה	עוֹנִי	מִצְוָה	רְצוֹנֶךָ
2.	רָצוֹן	צוֹדֵק	מִצְוֹתַי	לִרְצוֹן	עֲוֹנֹתַי
3.	וְצִוָּנוּ	בְּמִצְוֹת	מִצְרַיִם	אֲרָצוֹת	בְּמִצְוֹתָיו
4.	עֲוֹן	מַצוֹת	צוֹפִיָּה	צוֹרֶךְ	מְצוֹרָע
5.	בְּמִצְוֹתַי	מִצְוֹת	עֲוֹנָה	צַוָּה	מִצִּיּוֹן

Jewish prayer is a shared experience.

בִּרְכוֹת שֶׁל שַׁבָּת 3

"There is a realm of time where the goal is not to have but to be, not to own but to give, not to control but to share, not to subdue but to be in accord. Six days a week we live under the tyranny of things of space; on the Sabbath we try to become attuned to holiness in time."

— ABRAHAM JOSHUA HESCHEL, *THE SABBATH*

PRACTICE:

Read the three בְּרָכוֹת we say to welcome Shabbat.

בָּרוּךְ אַתָּה,	Blessed are You,
יְיָ אֱלֹהֵינוּ,	Adonai our God,
מֶלֶךְ הָעוֹלָם,	Sovereign of the universe,
אֲשֶׁר קִדְּשָׁנוּ	who makes us holy
בְּמִצְוֹתָיו	with commandments
וְצִוָּנוּ לְהַדְלִיק	and commands us to light
נֵר שֶׁל שַׁבָּת.	the Sabbath light (candles).

בָּרוּךְ אַתָּה,	Blessed are You,
יְיָ אֱלֹהֵינוּ,	Adonai our God,
מֶלֶךְ הָעוֹלָם,	Sovereign of the universe,
בּוֹרֵא	who creates
פְּרִי הַגָּפֶן.	the fruit of the vine.

בָּרוּךְ אַתָּה,	Blessed are You,
יְיָ אֱלֹהֵינוּ,	Adonai our God,
מֶלֶךְ הָעוֹלָם,	Sovereign of the universe,
הַמּוֹצִיא לֶחֶם	who brings forth bread
מִן הָאָרֶץ.	from the earth.

Lighting the Candles

We can welcome Shabbat into our homes with special acts and בְּרָכוֹת that usher us across the invisible threshold dividing the everyday from the holy. As a gavel declares that court is in session, and the lighting of the torch that the Olympic games have begun, so the lighting of the candles heralds the arrival of Shabbat.

בָּרוּךְ אַתָּה,	Blessed are You,
יְיָ אֱלֹהֵינוּ,	Adonai our God,
מֶלֶךְ הָעוֹלָם,	Sovereign of the universe,
אֲשֶׁר קִדְּשָׁנוּ	who makes us holy
בְּמִצְוֹתָיו וְצִוָּנוּ	with commandments and commands us
לְהַדְלִיק נֵר שֶׁל שַׁבָּת.	to light the Sabbath light (candles).

Lighting candles at the start of Shabbat and holidays is an act of sharing. As soon as a candle is lit, the light cannot be kept to one person; rather, the glow and radiance of the candles are shared with all those present.

PRACTICE:

Read the בְּרָכָה for lighting Shabbat candles.

PRAYER DICTIONARY

לְהַדְלִיק
to light

נֵר
a light, candle

שֶׁל
from, of

שַׁבָּת
Shabbat

A beautiful table can enrich the mitzvah of celebrating Shabbat.

Did You Know?

The Torah offers two versions of the commandment to observe Shabbat. In one *(Deuteronomy 5:12)*, we are told: שָׁמוֹר ("keep") the Sabbath day. In the other *(Exodus 20:8)*, we are told זָכוֹר ("remember") the Sabbath day. One speaks to the body, the other to the soul; one to the act, the other to the intent.

The kabbalists — Jewish mystics — say that the two candles represent the masculine and feminine aspects of God that unite on Shabbat, giving us a time of harmony and joy.

Some households light a candle for each member of the family. While traditionally women light the Shabbat candles, men can light them, too.

We light the Shabbat candles, then say the blessing while covering our eyes, as if to hide the flames.

Candles and Light

Candles can seem magical. The light of their wicks transforms the spaces we are in, reflecting the light that can soothe and comfort our spirits. We light candles at the beginning of Shabbat and during *havdalah* at its end. We light them on every major holiday and throughout the week of Ḥanukkah. We light a candle during the week of *shiva*, on days we say Yizkor (the memorial prayer for the dead), and when we observe *yahrzeit* (the anniversary of a loved one's death). In the Book of Psalms, God and Torah are both called "lamp" and "light." And an image of the seven-branched menorah that stood in the Temple two thousand years ago serves today as Israel's national symbol.

PRACTICE:

Read each of these blessings recited over candles.

Shabbat

בָּרוּךְ אַתָּה, יְיָ אֱלֹהֵינוּ, מֶלֶךְ הָעוֹלָם,
אֲשֶׁר קִדְּשָׁנוּ בְּמִצְוֹתָיו וְצִוָּנוּ לְהַדְלִיק נֵר שֶׁל שַׁבָּת.

Holiday

בָּרוּךְ אַתָּה, יְיָ אֱלֹהֵינוּ, מֶלֶךְ הָעוֹלָם,
אֲשֶׁר קִדְּשָׁנוּ בְּמִצְוֹתָיו וְצִוָּנוּ לְהַדְלִיק נֵר שֶׁל יוֹם טוֹב.

Shabbat and Holiday

בָּרוּךְ אַתָּה, יְיָ אֱלֹהֵינוּ, מֶלֶךְ הָעוֹלָם,
אֲשֶׁר קִדְּשָׁנוּ בְּמִצְוֹתָיו וְצִוָּנוּ לְהַדְלִיק
נֵר שֶׁל שַׁבָּת וְשֶׁל יוֹם טוֹב.

Ḥanukkah

בָּרוּךְ אַתָּה, יְיָ אֱלֹהֵינוּ, מֶלֶךְ הָעוֹלָם,
אֲשֶׁר קִדְּשָׁנוּ בְּמִצְוֹתָיו וְצִוָּנוּ לְהַדְלִיק נֵר שֶׁל חֲנֻכָּה.

Havdalah

בָּרוּךְ אַתָּה, יְיָ אֱלֹהֵינוּ, מֶלֶךְ הָעוֹלָם, בּוֹרֵא מְאוֹרֵי הָאֵשׁ.

Food for Thought

Most בְּרָכוֹת שֶׁל מִצְוָה are recited before the act to come, focusing our attention and consecrating the act. But the practice for Shabbat candles is different. First we light, and then we say the blessing. We reverse the order because, once we recite the blessing, it is as if Shabbat has begun. But if that were so, traditionally we would not be able to light the candles, for the Torah prohibits making fire on Shabbat. So we light the candles first, and cover our eyes, as if to hide the flames. When we open our eyes after reciting the blessing, it is as if the candles were just now kindled.

Blessing the Children

On Friday evening at the Shabbat table, some parents bless their children. Traditionally, they lightly place their hands on the child's head while reciting the following blessing:

For Sons

יְשִׂמְךָ אֱלֹהִים May God make you
כְּאֶפְרַיִם וְכִמְנַשֶּׁה. like Ephraim and Menasseh.

For Daughters

יְשִׂמֵךְ אֱלֹהִים May God make you
כְּשָׂרָה רִבְקָה רָחֵל וְלֵאָה. like Sarah, Rebecca, Rachel, and Leah.

The blessing concludes with the words recited by the priests who served in the ancient Temple about two thousand years ago. Though the blessing calls for the people of Israel to be blessed, it is written in the singular, indicating that each individual Jew is being blessed.

יְבָרֶכְךָ יְיָ וְיִשְׁמְרֶךָ. May God bless you and keep you.

יָאֵר יְיָ פָּנָיו אֵלֶיךָ May God's face shine upon you
וִיחֻנֶּךָּ. and be gracious to you.

יִשָּׂא יְיָ פָּנָיו אֵלֶיךָ May God's face be lifted to you
וְיָשֵׂם לְךָ שָׁלוֹם. and may God grant you peace.

Why do you think it is especially appropriate for parents to say these words to their children?

קִדּוּשׁ

Just as the Sabbath sanctifies us, so do we sanctify it. With a full cup of wine symbolizing overflowing joy and blessings, we recite the קִדּוּשׁ, the prayer that blesses this unique day. The prayer speaks of God's love for us, of Creation, and of the Exodus from Egypt. It tells us how Shabbat, above all else, was the first of all things in time or place to be called "holy."

The קִדּוּשׁ is recited both in synagogue and in the home. This custom began almost two thousand years ago, when the synagogue also served as a Jewish hostel. Travelers and visitors would spend the night in a side room, eating their meals as well as sleeping there. To be certain they fulfilled the mitzvah of hearing קִדּוּשׁ, the congregation recited the prayer in the synagogue.

PRACTICE:

Read the קִדּוּשׁ.

בָּרוּךְ אַתָּה, יְיָ אֱלֹהֵינוּ,	Blessed are You, Adonai our God,
מֶלֶךְ הָעוֹלָם,	Sovereign of the universe,
בּוֹרֵא פְּרִי הַגָּפֶן.	who creates the fruit of the vine.
בָּרוּךְ אַתָּה, יְיָ אֱלֹהֵינוּ,	Blessed are You, Adonai our God,
מֶלֶךְ הָעוֹלָם,	Sovereign of the universe,
אֲשֶׁר קִדְּשָׁנוּ בְּמִצְוֹתָיו	who makes us holy with commandments
וְרָצָה בָנוּ,	and takes delight in us.
וְשַׁבַּת קָדְשׁוֹ	God has made the holy Sabbath
בְּאַהֲבָה וּבְרָצוֹן הִנְחִילָנוּ,	our heritage in love and favor,
זִכָּרוֹן לְמַעֲשֵׂה בְרֵאשִׁית.	as a memory of the work of creation.
כִּי הוּא יוֹם תְּחִלָּה	It is first
לְמִקְרָאֵי קֹדֶשׁ,	among our holy days,
זֵכֶר לִיצִיאַת מִצְרָיִם.	a memory of the going out from Egypt.
כִּי בָנוּ בָחַרְתָּ	You chose us
וְאוֹתָנוּ קִדַּשְׁתָּ מִכָּל הָעַמִּים,	from all the nations and You made us holy.
וְשַׁבַּת קָדְשְׁךָ	You have given us the Sabbath
בְּאַהֲבָה וּבְרָצוֹן	in (with) love and favor
הִנְחַלְתָּנוּ.	as a sacred inheritance.
בָּרוּךְ אַתָּה יְיָ,	Blessed are You, Adonai,
מְקַדֵּשׁ הַשַּׁבָּת.	who makes the Sabbath holy.

19

At the Root

Words built on the root זכר have "remember" or "memory" as part of their meaning. Circle the root letters in the following words:

זִכָּרוֹן   יִזְכּוֹר   זֵכֶר

What two events do we recall in the Kiddush and why do you think each is significant?

1. _____

   _____

   _____

   _____

2. _____

   _____

   _____

   _____

An Ethical Echo

The concept of the Jews as the people chosen by God is complicated, even problematic, for many. The Reconstructionist movement omits phrases in its liturgy referring to the Jews' chosenness. But perhaps if we understand "chosen" in the sense of "beloved," we can maintain our special, chosen relationship with God and not deny others their own relationships with the divine.

How do you feel about the concept of "chosenness" in Judaism?

_____

_____

_____

_____

_____

PRAYER DICTIONARY

קִדוּשׁ
sanctification

זִכָּרוֹן
memory

(ל) מַעֲשֵׂה בְרֵאשִׁית
work of creation

זֵכֶר
memory

(ל) יְצִיאַת מִצְרָיִם
going out from Egypt

בְּאַהֲבָה
in (with) love

וּבְרָצוֹן
and in (with) favor

קִדּוּשׁ

"sanctification"

We know that the root letters קדשׁ קדשׁ mean "holy."

קִדּוּשׁ means "sanctification" (the act of making something holy).

קִדּוּשׁ helps make שַׁבָּת holy.

The following words all appear in the קִדּוּשׁ.

Circle the three root letters in each word. Read the words aloud.

מְקַדֵּשׁ   קָדְשְׁךָ   קִדַּשְׁתָּ   קֹדֶשׁ   קִדְּשׁוֹ   קִדְּשָׁנוּ

How does the קִדּוּשׁ help make שַׁבָּת holy?

_____

_____

_____

_____

The קִדּוּשׁ helps us remember events in our history that are reasons for joy.

One event is mentioned in these words from the קִדּוּשׁ:

זִכָּרוֹן לְמַעֲשֵׂה בְרֵאשִׁית

memory of the work of creation

Another event is found in the following words from the קִדּוּשׁ:

זֵכֶר לִיצִיאַת מִצְרָיִם

memory of the going out from Egypt

(ל)מַעֲשֵׂה בְּרֵאשִׁית

"work of creation"

When we say קָדוֹשׁ we remember two important events. One of them is the creation of the world.

מַעֲשֵׂה means "work of."

בְּרֵאשִׁית means "creation" (in the beginning).

בְּרֵאשִׁית is also the Hebrew name for Genesis, the first book of the תּוֹרָה.

Which of the following is *not* a meaning of בְּרֵאשִׁית? Circle it.

creation   Torah   Genesis   in the beginning

Draw a circle around the Hebrew word that means "the work of."

זִכָּרוֹן לְמַעֲשֵׂה בְּרֵאשִׁית

Underline the Hebrew word that means "creation."

(ל)יצִיאַת מִצְרַיִם

"going out from Egypt"

The second important event we remember in the קָדוֹשׁ is the going out from Egypt.

יְצִיאַת means "going out from."

מִצְרַיִם means "Egypt."

Draw a circle around the Hebrew word that means "going out from."

זֵכֶר לִיצִיאַת מִצְרַיִם

Underline the Hebrew word that means "Egypt."

בְּאַהֲבָה

"in (with) love"

בְּאַהֲבָה means "in (with) love."

בְּאַהֲבָה is made up of two parts:

בְּ at the beginning of a word means "in" or "with."

אַהֲבָה means "love."

Circle the prefix that means "in" or "with" in: בְּאַהֲבָה

וּבְרָצוֹן

"and in (with) favor"

וּבְרָצוֹן means "and in (with) favor."

וּבְרָצוֹן is made up of three parts:

וּ means "and."

בְ at the beginning of a word means "in" or "with."

רָצוֹן means "favor."

Circle the prefix that means "and" in: וּבְרָצוֹן

Wine, in moderation, gladdens the heart and enhances all Jewish celebrations.

Blessing over the Bread

It is in this blessing that the partnership between God and humanity is most evident. Making bread requires grain from the earth, wisdom from experience, and technology from human inventiveness. Just as we rely on God to help feed the world, so God relies on us. Perhaps that is why, among all the various blessings over fruits and drinks and vegetables, only the blessing over bread covers all the food to be eaten at a meal.

PRACTICE:
Read הַמּוֹצִיא.

בָּרוּךְ אַתָּה, יְיָ אֱלֹהֵינוּ,
מֶלֶךְ הָעוֹלָם,
הַמּוֹצִיא לֶחֶם מִן הָאָרֶץ.

Blessed are You, Adonai our God,
Sovereign of the universe,
who brings forth bread from the earth.

An Ethical Echo

"The Bible is more concerned with time [and how we fill it] than with space .... It pays more attention to generations [and] to events, than to countries [and] to things .... Judaism teaches us to be attached to holiness in time, to be attached to sacred events, to learn how to consecrate sanctuaries that emerge from the magnificent stream of a year."

— ABRAHAM JOSHUA HESCHEL, *THE SABBATH*

How do you think the rest of the week feels if you know you have a day off every Shabbat?

_____

_____

_____

BUILDING YOUR VOCABULARY

The concluding words of the blessing over bread are "who brings forth bread from the earth." Draw a line to connect these words to the corresponding Hebrew.

who brings forth	מִן
bread	הָאָרֶץ
from	לֶחֶם
the earth	הַמּוֹצִיא

PRAYER DICTIONARY

הַמּוֹצִיא
who brings forth

לֶחֶם
bread

מִן
from

הָאָרֶץ
the earth

הַבְדָּלָה

After the sun sets, when we can see three medium-sized stars in the sky, Shabbat ends. We escort it out with a special service called הַבְדָּלָה ("separation," "differentiation"). Using a tall, braided candle with two or more wicks, a container with spices (cloves and cinnamon are popular choices), and a cup of wine, we make the transition from Shabbat back to the rough-and-tumble everyday world. The theme is distinctions: distinguishing sacred time from mundane time, night from day, Shabbat from the workweek.

PRACTICE:

Read the blessings for הַבְדָּלָה.

בָּרוּךְ אַתָּה,	Blessed are You,
יְיָ אֱלֹהֵינוּ,	Adonai our God,
מֶלֶךְ הָעוֹלָם,	Sovereign of the universe,
בּוֹרֵא פְּרִי הַגָּפֶן.	who creates the fruit of the vine.
בָּרוּךְ אַתָּה,	Blessed are You,
יְיָ אֱלֹהֵינוּ,	Adonai our God,
מֶלֶךְ הָעוֹלָם,	Sovereign of the universe,
בּוֹרֵא מִינֵי בְשָׂמִים.	who creates the varieties of spice.
בָּרוּךְ אַתָּה,	Blessed are You,
יְיָ אֱלֹהֵינוּ,	Adonai our God,
מֶלֶךְ הָעוֹלָם,	Sovereign of the universe,
בּוֹרֵא מְאוֹרֵי הָאֵשׁ.	who creates the fiery lights.
בָּרוּךְ אַתָּה,	Blessed are You,
יְיָ אֱלֹהֵינוּ,	Adonai our God,
מֶלֶךְ הָעוֹלָם,	Sovereign of the universe,
הַמַּבְדִּיל בֵּין קֹדֶשׁ לְחוֹל,	who separates the holy from the everyday,
בֵּין אוֹר לְחשֶׁךְ,	light from darkness,
בֵּין יוֹם הַשְּׁבִיעִי	the seventh day
לְשֵׁשֶׁת יְמֵי הַמַּעֲשֶׂה.	from the six days of work.
בָּרוּךְ אַתָּה יְיָ,	Blessed are You, Adonai,
הַמַּבְדִּיל בֵּין קֹדֶשׁ לְחוֹל.	who separates the holy from the everyday.

בִּרְכוֹת שֶׁל יוֹם טוֹב

Every holiday has its own values, rituals, and store of blessings. Most holidays begin with two blessings: candlelighting and the שֶׁהֶחֱיָנוּ blessing. If the holiday falls on Shabbat, then during the candlelighting blessing, reference to Shabbat comes first. This follows a standard rule for ritual practice: If two elements are to be mentioned in one blessing, and one occurs more often than the other (in this case, Shabbat occurs more often than the holiday), the one that occurs more often comes first.

It is a solution to the question we all sometimes face: Which should receive the place of honor, the one whose presence is rare or the one whose presence is steadfast? In the case of the blessing, Judaism opts for the steadfast.

Rosh Hashanah and Yom Kippur

בָּרוּךְ אַתָּה, יְיָ אֱלֹהֵינוּ,
Blessed are You, Adonai our God,

מֶלֶךְ הָעוֹלָם,
Sovereign of the universe,

אֲשֶׁר קִדְּשָׁנוּ בְּמִצְוֹתָיו
who makes us holy with commandments

וְצִוָּנוּ לְהַדְלִיק
and commands us to light

נֵר שֶׁל (שַׁבָּת וְשֶׁל) יוֹם טוֹב.
(the Sabbath and) the holiday light (candles).

PRACTICE:

Read the blessings for Rosh Hashanah.

Candlelighting is often followed by the recitation of the שֶׁהֶחֱיָנוּ, the blessing of appreciation. We say it when we graduate from school, receive an honor, and reach a milestone, and on the first night of almost every holiday.

בָּרוּךְ אַתָּה, יְיָ אֱלֹהֵינוּ,
Blessed are You, Adonai our God,

מֶלֶךְ הָעוֹלָם,
Sovereign of the universe,

שֶׁהֶחֱיָנוּ וְקִיְּמָנוּ
who has given us life, sustained us,

וְהִגִּיעָנוּ לַזְּמַן הַזֶּה.
and enabled us to reach this time.

26

On Rosh Hashanah, this blessing is often accompanied by eating a new fruit of the season, in addition to the tradition of eating apples and honey. Some families choose a pomegranate, for it symbolizes fullness and plenty, youth and energy, fairly bursting as it is with hundreds of seeds.

PRACTICE:

Read the blessing over fruit.

בָּרוּךְ אַתָּה, יְיָ אֱלֹהֵינוּ,
Blessed are You, Adonai our God,

מֶלֶךְ הָעוֹלָם,
Sovereign of the universe,

בּוֹרֵא פְּרִי הָעֵץ.
who creates the fruit of the tree.

What is the tradition in your family? What fruit do you eat on Rosh Hashanah?

PRACTICE:

Read the candlelighting blessing for Yom Kippur.

Yom Kippur begins with its own unique candlelighting blessing. (Only Yom Kippur, Ḥanukkah, and Shabbat, of all the holidays, are specifically mentioned by name in candlelighting blessings.)

בָּרוּךְ אַתָּה, יְיָ אֱלֹהֵינוּ,
Blessed are You, Adonai our God,

מֶלֶךְ הָעוֹלָם,
Sovereign of the universe,

אֲשֶׁר קִדְּשָׁנוּ בְּמִצְוֹתָיו
who makes us holy with commandments

וְצִוָּנוּ לְהַדְלִיק נֵר שֶׁל
and commands us to light (the Sabbath and)

(שַׁבָּת וְשֶׁל) יוֹם הַכִּפּוּרִים.
the Yom Kippur light (candles).

The shofar's call conjures up the voice of God and the voice of the Jewish people. We can almost imagine the three distinct sounds of the shofar as a conversation with God. The sounds are: *t'ki'ah*, one long blast; *sh'varim*, three broken, rising blasts; and *t'ru'ah*, nine short calls.

Every day throughout the month of Elul — the last month of the Jewish calendar — the shofar is blown at the end of morning prayers. On Rosh Hashanah, the first, single, sustained, primitive *t'ki'ah* explodes, sounding as if it might be a call from beyond, piercing our spiritual armor. We respond with the plaintive *sh'varim*. The ninefold staccato blasts of the *t'ru'ah* are the blending of our cries with God's. And the final *t'ki'ah* could be construed as God's acceptance of our prayer.

PRACTICE:

Read the blessing before the blowing of the shofar.

בָּרוּךְ אַתָּה, יְיָ אֱלֹהֵינוּ,
Blessed are You, Adonai our God,

מֶלֶךְ הָעוֹלָם,
Sovereign of the universe,

אֲשֶׁר קִדְּשָׁנוּ בְּמִצְוֹתָיו
who makes us holy with commandments

וְצִוָּנוּ לִשְׁמֹעַ קוֹל שׁוֹפָר.
and commands us to hear the sound of the shofar.

Sukkot

Sukkot is a sensory experience. We smell the citrus scent of the *etrog*, hear the rustle as we shake the *lulav*, and experience nature by being outdoors as we dwell in the sukkah.

When we eat in the sukkah, we begin each meal with a blessing of mitzvah.

PRACTICE:

Read the blessing for sitting in the sukkah.

בָּרוּךְ אַתָּה, יְיָ אֱלֹהֵינוּ,

Blessed are You, Adonai our God,

מֶלֶךְ הָעוֹלָם,

Sovereign of the universe,

אֲשֶׁר קִדְּשָׁנוּ בְּמִצְוֹתָיו

who makes us holy with commandments

וְצִוָּנוּ לֵישֵׁב בַּסֻּכָּה.

and commands us to sit in the sukkah.

On Sukkot we reenact an ancient ritual involving the *lulav* and *etrog* — the four species that represent both the fertility of the land of Israel and God's presence throughout the world. The *etrog* is a citrus fruit, looking and smelling much like a large lemon. It is nice to hold, lovely to see, refreshing to smell, and, when cooked right, tasty to eat. Given all of these attributes, one midrash tells us that the forbidden fruit that Eve ate in the Garden was not an apple but an *etrog*.

The *lulav* is made of up of three plants: the palm, which serves as the spine and foundation of the *lulav*; the willow, which adorns the palm on the left side, and the myrtle, which adorns the palm on the right. Together, the *lulav* and *etrog* represent the fertility of the land of Israel. Every day of the holiday (except on Shabbat) they are held in both hands and shaken in all directions, encompassing all the directions of the world (east, south, west, north, up, down).

A *lulav* and an *etrog*

PRACTICE:

Read the blessing over the *lulav* and *etrog*.

בָּרוּךְ אַתָּה, יְיָ אֱלֹהֵינוּ,
מֶלֶךְ הָעוֹלָם,
אֲשֶׁר קִדְּשָׁנוּ בְּמִצְוֹתָיו
וְצִוָּנוּ עַל נְטִילַת לוּלָב.

Blessed are You, Adonai our God,
Sovereign of the universe,
who makes us holy with commandments
and commands us to shake the *lulav*.

Sukkot symbolizes the fragility of life by commanding us to dwell outdoors in a temporary structure — the sukkah. In what way is being in a sukkah similar to and different from being in a tent, or having a camping experience?

_____

_____

_____

_____

_____

We decorate the sukkah with fruits and vegetables that remind us of the fall harvest.

Ḥanukkah

Ḥanukkah is a celebration of light. We light candles on each of the eight nights while reciting two blessings. The first is the blessing of mitzvah, when we state our intention to fulfill the commandment to light the candles. The second is a blessing of awe and gratitude, when we bind today, this moment in time, to the miracle of the Maccabees so many years ago. On the first night of Ḥanukkah, we follow these two blessings with the שֶׁהֶחֱיָנוּ.

PRACTICE:

Read the blessings for lighting the Ḥanukkah candles.

בָּרוּךְ אַתָּה, יְיָ אֱלֹהֵינוּ,	Blessed are You, Adonai our God,

מֶלֶךְ הָעוֹלָם,	Sovereign of the universe,

אֲשֶׁר קִדְּשָׁנוּ בְּמִצְוֹתָיו	who makes us holy with commandments

וְצִוָּנוּ לְהַדְלִיק	and commands us to light

נֵר שֶׁל חֲנֻכָּה.	the Ḥanukkah candles.

בָּרוּךְ אַתָּה, יְיָ אֱלֹהֵינוּ,	Blessed are You, Adonai our God,

מֶלֶךְ הָעוֹלָם,	Sovereign of the universe,

שֶׁעָשָׂה נִסִּים לַאֲבוֹתֵינוּ	who made miracles for our ancestors

בַּיָּמִים הָהֵם בַּזְּמַן הַזֶּה.	long ago, at this season.

An Ethical Echo

Judaism speaks of two kinds of miracles: when the unexpected happens (such as the Red Sea parting after the Exodus from Egypt) and when the expected doesn't (when the burning bush was not consumed). It is hard to ignore the first kind but it is easy to miss the second. The rabbis ask: How long did Moses have to look at the bush before noticing that it was not burning up? And we in turn can ask ourselves: How many miracles have we overlooked, not pausing long enough to know what we were seeing?

What in your opinion constitutes a miracle?

_____

_____

_____

Pesaḥ

PRACTICE:

Read the blessings
we say during
the Passover seder.

The Passover seder is a meal full of prayers, questions, storytelling, and song. It is also a time of contrast. In the comfort of our homes, we recall our ancestors' homelessness in the desert; at a meal of plenty, we welcome in the hungry; in the atmosphere of freedom, we tell the stories of slavery.

On Drinking the Wine

בָּרוּךְ אַתָּה, יְיָ אֱלֹהֵינוּ,　Blessed are You, Adonai our God,

מֶלֶךְ הָעוֹלָם,　Sovereign of the universe,

בּוֹרֵא פְּרִי הַגָּפֶן.　who creates the fruit of the vine.

On Eating a Green Vegetable

בָּרוּךְ אַתָּה, יְיָ אֱלֹהֵינוּ,　Blessed are You, Adonai our God,

מֶלֶךְ הָעוֹלָם,　Sovereign of the universe,

בּוֹרֵא פְּרִי הָאֲדָמָה.　who creates the fruit of the earth.

On Eating the Matzah

בָּרוּךְ אַתָּה, יְיָ אֱלֹהֵינוּ,　Blessed are You, Adonai our God,

מֶלֶךְ הָעוֹלָם,　Sovereign of the universe,

הַמּוֹצִיא לֶחֶם מִן הָאָרֶץ.　who brings forth bread from the earth.

בָּרוּךְ אַתָּה, יְיָ אֱלֹהֵינוּ,　Blessed are You, Adonai our God,

מֶלֶךְ הָעוֹלָם,　Sovereign of the universe,

אֲשֶׁר קִדְּשָׁנוּ בְּמִצְוֹתָיו　who makes us holy with commandments

וְצִוָּנוּ עַל אֲכִילַת מַצָּה.　and commands us to eat matzah.

On Eating Bitter Herbs

בָּרוּךְ אַתָּה, יְיָ אֱלֹהֵינוּ,　Blessed are You, Adonai our God,

מֶלֶךְ הָעוֹלָם,　Sovereign of the universe,

אֲשֶׁר קִדְּשָׁנוּ בְּמִצְוֹתָיו　who makes us holy with commandments

וְצִוָּנוּ עַל אֲכִילַת מָרוֹר.　and commands us to eat bitter herbs.

We are commanded to teach our children during the seder about the Exodus from Egypt, according to their own level of understanding, and to arouse each person's curiosity.

Name one way you have enlivened your seder or aroused the curiosity of those present.

בָּרְכוּ 5

"Those in prayer are like those who walk in a garden, plucking flowers one by one to weave a garland of color and fragrance. They enter the world of prayer moving from letter to letter, from word to word, plucking them and weaving a garland of song. The flowers adorn the body; the prayers adorn the spirit."

— *BASED ON RABBI NAHMAN OF BRATZLAV*

As we enter the synagogue, the worries and distractions of the world still cling to our clothing and hang on our thoughts. Perhaps we want to be in services; perhaps we don't. Either way, there we are, and the leader calls us to order with the words:

PRACTICE:

Read the בָּרְכוּ.

בָּרְכוּ אֶת יְיָ הַמְבֹרָךְ.   Bless Adonai, who is to be blessed.

In that moment, we are invited to shed unwanted burdens, ease ourselves into a place of caring, and enter the garden of prayer.

The בָּרְכוּ is as old as Jewish prayer itself. Its first appearance occurs at the end of Psalms 135, when all Israel is called to praise God. The early rabbis of almost two thousand years ago borrowed this phrase and placed it at the beginning of every morning and evening service. Sometime soon thereafter, a ritualized response to the call to prayer developed. After all, how could one be called upon to praise God and not respond?

PRACTICE:

Read the response
to the בָּרְכוּ.

בָּרוּךְ יְיָ   Blessed is Adonai,

הַמְבֹרָךְ לְעוֹלָם וָעֶד.   who is to be blessed forever and ever.

PRAYER DICTIONARY

בָּרְכוּ
bless!

יְיָ
Adonai

הַמְבֹרָךְ
who is to be blessed

בָּרוּךְ
blessed, praised

לְעוֹלָם וָעֶד
forever and ever

BUILDING YOUR VOCABULARY

Circle the Hebrew word(s) that corresponds to the English.

forever and ever	אֶת	לְעוֹלָם וָעֶד	בָּרְכוּ
Adonai	יְיָ	בָּרְכוּ	בָּרוּךְ
bless!	אֶת	הַמְבֹרָךְ	בָּרְכוּ
who is to be blessed	הַמְבֹרָךְ	לְעוֹלָם וָעֶד	אֶת

בָּרְכוּ אֶת יְיָ הַמְבֹרָךְ.

Circle the words in the בָּרְכוּ with the root ברכ.

Hint: כ, כ, and ךְ are related letters, as are ב and בּ.

What is the general meaning of words built on this root? _____

RELATED LETTERS

The words below contain related letters: ב בּ and כ כ ךְ.
Practice reading them.

.1	כ ךְ	כָּמוֹךְ	יָדְךָ	לָךְ	כָּל	תּוֹכֵנוּ	מֶלֶךְ
.2	כּ כ	מְכַלְכֵּל	כְּמַלְכֵּנוּ	כָּמְכָה	מִכָּל	אָכַל	כָּל
.3	בּ ב	אֲבָל	כּוֹכָבִים	בִּדְבָרוֹ	בַּלֵּבָב	מַכַּבִּי	בְּבֵית

Think About It!

The בָּרְכוּ is also part of the blessing said before the reading of the Torah. It is as if the one honored with the *aliyah* announces to the congregation when reciting the blessings, "I am ready. Are you?" And the congregation responds, "We are ready."

Why repeat the בָּרְכוּ in the Torah blessings? Because it is as if the Torah reading were a reenactment of the Revelation at Sinai. Even as the whole world was silent to hear the word of God there, so the congregation should be attentive to hear the word of God here.

PRACTICE:

Read the blessing before the Torah reading.

בָּרְכוּ אֶת יְיָ הַמְבֹרָךְ.   Bless Adonai, who is to be blessed.

בָּרוּךְ יְיָ הַמְבֹרָךְ   Blessed is Adonai, who is to be blessed

לְעוֹלָם וָעֶד.   forever and ever.

בָּרוּךְ אַתָּה, יְיָ אֱלֹהֵינוּ,   Blessed are You, Adonai our God,

מֶלֶךְ הָעוֹלָם,   sovereign of the world,

אֲשֶׁר בָּחַר בָּנוּ מִכָּל הָעַמִּים,   for choosing us from all the nations

וְנָתַן לָנוּ אֶת תּוֹרָתוֹ.   and giving us God's Torah.

בָּרוּךְ אַתָּה יְיָ,   Blessed are You, Adonai,

נוֹתֵן הַתּוֹרָה.   who gives us the Torah.

You will study the complete Torah blessings in Chapter 17 of this book.

A *sofer*, or scribe, carefully writes the letters in a Torah scroll using a quill pen and special black ink.

God's Name

Tradition tells us that God has seventy-two names — הָרַחֲמָן ("the Merciful One"), צוּר ("the Rock"), הַמָּקוֹם ("the Place"), and אֵל שַׁדַּי ("El Shaddai") among them. In most prayer books, however, God is called יְהֹוָה or אֱלֹהִים. And while אֱלֹהִים is pronounced as it is written, יְהֹוָה is not. Rather, it is pronounced Adonai. In the days of the ancient Temple, only once a year, on Yom Kippur, did the High Priest speak God's name, יְהֹוָה. And it is never written except in the context of prayer and Torah. The mystery of the pronunciation of God's name is said to have been lost with the destruction of the Temple in 586 BCE.

Sometimes Adonai is written יְיָ or ה'. Either way, it is pronounced Adonai.

PRACTICE:

Read the sentences.
Circle God's name
wherever it appears.

1. בָּרְכוּ אֶת יְיָ הַמְבֹרָךְ.

2. בָּרוּךְ יְיָ הַמְבֹרָךְ לְעוֹלָם וָעֶד.

3. מֵאֵין כָּמוֹךָ, יְהֹוָה, גָּדוֹל אַתָּה וְגָדוֹל שִׁמְךָ בִּגְבוּרָה.

4. כִּי לְךָ ה' הַגְּדֻלָּה וְהַגְּבוּרָה וְהַתִּפְאֶרֶת.

5. יְיָ צְבָאוֹת שְׁמוֹ.

6. גָּדוֹל ה' וּמְהֻלָּל מְאֹד, וְלִגְדֻלָּתוֹ אֵין חֵקֶר.

Built in 1763, Touro Synagogue in Newport, Rhode Island is the oldest synagogue in America.

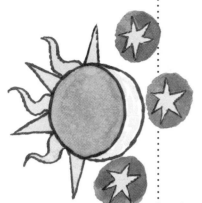

מַעֲרִיב עֲרָבִים ⬠6
יוֹצֵר אוֹר

מַעֲרִיב
עֲרָבִים

The Jewish day begins with sunset, replaying the works of creation, "and there was evening and there was morning, one day" *(GENESIS 1:5)*. With nightfall each day, we can review, as God did, the work of the previous day, and we can imagine for ourselves the possibilities that await us tomorrow.

But so often we don't. Time and distraction conspire against such luxuries as stepping back, quieting down, being reflective. Speaking the words of the מַעֲרִיב slows us down. The prayer unhurriedly repeats itself, easing the rush and the urgency of now, encouraging us to loosen our grip on the baggage of the day. It speaks of the gentle roll of time, guided by the will of God. Perspective, it calls to us, and purpose. Do not believe that there is a clock but no clockmaker. Time is in God's hands.

PRACTICE:

Read
מַעֲרִיב עֲרָבִים.

בָּרוּךְ אַתָּה, יְיָ אֱלֹהֵינוּ,	Blessed are You, Adonai our God,
מֶלֶךְ הָעוֹלָם,	Sovereign of the universe,
אֲשֶׁר בִּדְבָרוֹ	whose word
מַעֲרִיב עֲרָבִים,	brings on the evening
בְּחָכְמָה	and who, with wisdom,
פּוֹתֵחַ שְׁעָרִים,	opens the gates (of heaven),
וּבִתְבוּנָה מְשַׁנֶּה עִתִּים,	and changes times with understanding,
וּמַחֲלִיף אֶת הַזְּמַנִּים,	and varies the seasons,
וּמְסַדֵּר אֶת הַכּוֹכָבִים,	and who arranges the stars
בְּמִשְׁמְרוֹתֵיהֶם בָּרָקִיעַ	in their stations in the firmament (sky)
כִּרְצוֹנוֹ.	according to God's will.

 continued

מַעֲרִיב עֲרָבִים
brings on the evening

חַי
living, lives

וְקַיָּם
and eternal

יִמְלֹךְ
will rule

בּוֹרֵא יוֹם וָלָיְלָה,	Creator of day and night,
גּוֹלֵל אוֹר מִפְּנֵי חֹשֶׁךְ,	who rolls light away from darkness
וְחֹשֶׁךְ מִפְּנֵי אוֹר,	and darkness away from light,
וּמַעֲבִיר יוֹם	and who causes the day to pass
וּמֵבִיא לָיְלָה,	and brings on night,
וּמַבְדִּיל בֵּין יוֹם וּבֵין לָיְלָה,	and who divides between day and night,
יְיָ צְבָאוֹת שְׁמוֹ.	Adonai of Hosts is God's name.
אֵל חַי וְקַיָּם,	Living and enduring God,
תָּמִיד יִמְלֹךְ עָלֵינוּ	rule over us
לְעוֹלָם וָעֶד.	forever and ever.
בָּרוּךְ אַתָּה יְיָ,	Blessed are You, Adonai,
הַמַּעֲרִיב עֲרָבִים.	who brings on evening.

At the Root

עֶרֶב means "evening." According to *midrash* (commentary on the Torah), the Jewish day begins at sundown because the moon and stars were created before the sun. Therefore, each Jewish day is counted from sunset to sunset and each Jewish holiday begins in the evening. For example, the evening when Rosh Hashanah begins is called עֶרֶב רֹאשׁ הַשָּׁנָה.

The two words in the phrase מַעֲרִיב עֲרָבִים share the root ערב. Many words built on this root have "evening" as part of their meaning.

Circle the three root letters in each word: מַעֲרִיב עֲרָבִים

Think About It!

Why do you think the prayer begins and ends with the same statement that God brings on the evening?

_____

_____

יוֹצֵר אוֹר

On the other side of the night we wake up with a fresh start. Just as we spoke of God's hand in bringing us nightfall, so we acknowledge God's hand in bringing us daylight. First recited as long ago as the time of the Second Temple, about five hundred years before the Common Era, this morning prayer recalls two forms of light: the renewed light (אוֹר חָדָשׁ) of Creation, which we are privileged to enjoy every day, and the new light that represents the age of redemption, the messianic era.

PRACTICE:

Read יוֹצֵר אוֹר.

בָּרוּךְ אַתָּה,	Blessed are You,
יְיָ אֱלֹהֵינוּ,	Adonai our God,
מֶלֶךְ הָעוֹלָם,	Sovereign of the universe,
יוֹצֵר אוֹר, וּבוֹרֵא חֹשֶׁךְ,	who forms light and creates darkness,
עֹשֶׂה שָׁלוֹם	who makes peace
וּבוֹרֵא אֶת הַכֹּל.	and creates all things.
אוֹר חָדָשׁ עַל צִיּוֹן תָּאִיר	Cause a new light to shine on Zion,
וְנִזְכֶּה כֻלָּנוּ מְהֵרָה לְאוֹרוֹ.	and may all of us be worthy to see its light.
בָּרוּךְ אַתָּה יְיָ,	Blessed are You, Adonai,
יוֹצֵר הַמְּאוֹרוֹת.	the Creator of lights.

אוֹר means "light." In previous chapters, we learned the word נֵר, also meaning "light" or "candle." (. . . לְהַדְלִיק נֵר שֶׁל)

In what way could אוֹר and נֵר be interpreted as different forms of "light"?

_____

_____

_____

Light It Up

Circle the common letters in the following two words: אוֹר הַמְּאוֹרוֹת

The Torah teaches that God created the sun, moon, and stars on the fourth day of Creation, but God created light on the first day.

What do you think the light was like before God created the sun, moon, and stars?

_____

_____

At the Root

In praising God as Creator, יוֹצֵר אוֹר uses three verbs having to do with "making new" — "forms," "creates," and "makes."

יוֹצֵר אוֹר	forms light
וּבוֹרֵא חֹשֶׁךְ	and creates darkness
עֹשֶׂה שָׁלוֹם	makes peace
וּבוֹרֵא אֶת הַכֹּל	and creates all things

The root of וּבוֹרֵא is ברא ("create"). The first line of the first book of the Torah (בְּרֵאשִׁית) includes the word בָּרָא.

בְּרֵאשִׁית בָּרָא אֱלֹהִים	In the beginning God created
אֵת הַשָּׁמַיִם וְאֵת הָאָרֶץ . . .	the heavens and the earth . . . .

Why do you think יוֹצֵר אוֹר not only acknowledges God as Sovereign of the Universe, Former of Light, Creator of Darkness, Creator of All Things, but also Maker of Peace?

_____

_____

_____

שְׁמַע  7

The שְׁמַע is so much more than a prayer. It is a badge, a banner, a symbol of Judaism. In addition to saying it in the evening and morning services, we recite it before going to bed, when we take the Torah out of the Ark, in the additional service on Shabbat and holidays, at the very end of Yom Kippur, and on the deathbed. We enclose portions of it in our *mezuzot*, hang it on our doorposts, and wear it in tefillin.

Elie Wiesel tells a story about the camps. It was the holiday of Simḥat Torah, when Jews traditionally dance with the Torah. Having no Torah around, an old man turned to a young child and asked: Did you learn the שְׁמַע? The child said yes, and the old man picked him up and danced with him.

PRACTICE:

Read the שְׁמַע.

שְׁמַע יִשְׂרָאֵל: Hear O Israel:

יְיָ אֱלֹהֵינוּ,   Adonai is our God,

יְיָ אֶחָד.   Adonai is One.

— *Deuteronomy 6:4*

An Ethical Echo

"There are three crowns: the crown of Torah, the crown of priesthood, and the crown of royalty. But the crown of a good name exceeds them all."

— *Pirkei Avot 4:17*

All the details of our lives are captured by that most modest of possessions, our name. All that we do, all that we believe, all that we champion or decline to champion resonate in the memory of our name. We might have been given our name by our parents, but we are the authors of the stories that fill it. The one possession beyond all others that is not relinquished even after we die is our name.

PRAYER DICTIONARY

שְׁמַע
hear

יִשְׂרָאֵל
Israel

יְיָ
Adonai

אֱלֹהֵינוּ
our God

אֶחָד
one

WHAT'S MISSING?

Fill in the missing English word on each line. Practice reading the Hebrew aloud.

1. שְׁמַע   _____O Israel

2. אֶחָד   Adonai is _____

3. יִשְׂרָאֵל   Hear O _____

4. יְיָ   _____ is our God

Witness to God

In the Torah, the ע of שְׁמַע and the ד of אֶחָד are written larger than the other letters. Together, these two letters form the word עֵד ("witness"). Who is a witness to what? Perhaps the verse is a witness to the founding faith of our ancestors. Perhaps it asks us to serve as witnesses to God's singular presence. Perhaps it asks us to serve as witnesses to one another of our steadfast covenant with God or calls to God to witness our faithfulness. Perhaps the question is more important than the answer.

What do *you* think the שְׁמַע asks us to witness?

_____

_____

The שְׁמַע is often recited with quiet intensity.

Prayer Building Blocks

אֱלֹהֵינוּ

"our God"	אֱלֹהֵינוּ is made up of two parts:
	אֱלֹהֵי means "God of."
	נוּ means "us" or "our."

READING PRACTICE

Practice reading the following סִדּוּר phrases.

Circle the word אֱלֹהֵינוּ wherever it appears.

1. רְצֵה יְיָ אֱלֹהֵינוּ בְּעַמְּךָ יִשְׂרָאֵל.

2. בָּרֵךְ עָלֵינוּ, יְיָ אֱלֹהֵינוּ, אֵת הַשָּׁנָה הַזֹּאת.

3. אַהֲבָה רַבָּה אֲהַבְתָּנוּ, יְיָ אֱלֹהֵינוּ.

4. הַשְׁכִּיבֵנוּ יְיָ אֱלֹהֵינוּ לְשָׁלוֹם.

We hang the words of the שְׁמַע on our doorposts.

The Response

When the שְׁמַע became part of our prayer service about two thousand years ago, it was read responsively. The reader would call out the first two words, שְׁמַע יִשְׂרָאֵל, and the congregation would respond with the full line. The reader in turn would respond:

בָּרוּךְ שֵׁם כְּבוֹד מַלְכוּתוֹ לְעוֹלָם וָעֶד.

Blessed is the name of God's glorious kingdom forever and ever.

Today, everyone says both lines. But while the שְׁמַע is said with gusto, the response, בָּרוּךְ שֵׁם, is often said quietly. Explanations as to why vary, but perhaps the best is that it interrupts the flow of the Torah text, insinuating itself between the שְׁמַע (DEUTERONOMY 6:4) and וְאָהַבְתָּ (DEUTERONOMY 6:5).

שְׁמַע יִשְׂרָאֵל: יְיָ אֱלֹהֵינוּ, יְיָ אֶחָד.
בָּרוּךְ שֵׁם כְּבוֹד מַלְכוּתוֹ לְעוֹלָם וָעֶד.

PRACTICE:

Read both lines of the שְׁמַע aloud.

PRAYER DICTIONARY

בָּרוּךְ	blessed, praised
שֵׁם	name
כְּבוֹד	glory of
מַלְכוּתוֹ	God's kingdom
לְעוֹלָם וָעֶד	forever and ever

BUILDING YOUR VOCABULARY

Number the words in the correct order.

מַלְכוּתוֹ שֵׁם בָּרוּךְ וָעֶד לְעוֹלָם כְּבוֹד

Underline the word with the root מלכ.

What meaning does this root denote? _____

Circle the root מלכ in each of the words below:

מֶלֶךְ מַלְכֵּנוּ מַלְכוּת מַלְכָּה יִמְלֹךְ

וְאָהַבְתָּ 8

וְאָהַבְתָּ, which follows immediately after the שְׁמַע, commands us to "love Adonai, your God." You may wonder: How can we be commanded to love? How can we be commanded to feel *any* emotion? Here are two ways we might understand this prayer: The first is that the Torah is not commanding us to love, but commanding us to act *as if* we love. We know, in other areas of our lives, that when feelings fail, actions carry us through. We tell children to say they are sorry, even if they aren't, for, in acting that way, they might begin to feel that way.

The second grounds itself in semantics. In the biblical period, the word "love" often referred not to a feeling of affection, but to the willingness to enter into a relationship. To love God suggests a willingness to be one of God's people.

PRACTICE:

Read the וְאָהַבְתָּ.

וְאָהַבְתָּ אֵת יְיָ אֱלֹהֶיךָ,	You shall love Adonai, your God,
בְּכָל לְבָבְךָ וּבְכָל נַפְשְׁךָ	with all your heart, and with all your soul,
וּבְכָל מְאֹדֶךָ.	and with all your might.
וְהָיוּ הַדְּבָרִים הָאֵלֶּה,	Set these words,
אֲשֶׁר אָנֹכִי מְצַוְּךָ הַיּוֹם,	which I command you this day,
עַל לְבָבֶךָ.	upon your heart.
וְשִׁנַּנְתָּם לְבָנֶיךָ,	Teach them to your children,
וְדִבַּרְתָּ בָּם בְּשִׁבְתְּךָ בְּבֵיתֶךָ,	and speak of them when you are at home,
וּבְלֶכְתְּךָ בַדֶּרֶךְ	and when you go on your way,
וּבְשָׁכְבְּךָ וּבְקוּמֶךָ.	and when you lie down, and when you get up.
וּקְשַׁרְתָּם לְאוֹת עַל יָדֶךָ,	Bind them as a sign upon your hand
וְהָיוּ לְטֹטָפֹת בֵּין עֵינֶיךָ,	and let them be symbols between your eyes.
וּכְתַבְתָּם עַל מְזֻזוֹת	Write them on the doorposts
בֵּיתֶךָ וּבִשְׁעָרֶיךָ.	of your house and on your gates.

PRAYER DICTIONARY

וְאָהַבְתָּ
you shall love

לְבָבְךָ
your heart

הַדְּבָרִים
the words

לְאוֹת
as a sign

מְזֻזוֹת
mezuzot, doorposts

בֵּיתֶךָ
your house

BUILDING YOUR VOCABULARY

Write the translation of each Hebrew word.

1. _____ מְזֻזוֹת
2. _____ לְבָבְךָ
3. _____ בֵּיתֶךָ
4. _____ וְאָהַבְתָּ
5. _____ הַדְּבָרִים

At the Root

Below are the names of three prayers whose theme is the love between God and the Jewish people.

אַהֲבָה רַבָּה   אַהֲבַת עוֹלָם   וְאָהַבְתָּ

Within each name you will see the root letters אהב ("love").
Circle those letters.

Through the ethical mitzvot, we enter into loving relationships with others.

הַדְּבָרִים

"the words"

הַדְּבָרִים is made up of two parts:

הַ means "the."

דְּבָרִים means "words."

Circle the word part that means "the." הַדְּבָרִים

בֵּיתֶךָ

"your house"

The word בֵּיתֶךָ is made up of two parts:

בַּיִת means "house."

ךָ is an ending that means "you" or "your."

בֵּיתֶךָ means "your house."

(When we combine בַּיִת and ךָ, the word is written בֵּיתְךָ or בֵּיתֶךָ.)

There are many words in the וְאָהַבְתָּ with the ending ךָ.

Read the first three lines of the וְאָהַבְתָּ and circle each word with the ending ךָ.

1. וְאָהַבְתָּ אֵת יְיָ אֱלֹהֶיךָ

2. בְּכָל לְבָבְךָ וּבְכָל נַפְשְׁךָ וּבְכָל מְאֹדֶךָ.

3. וְהָיוּ הַדְּבָרִים הָאֵלֶּה, אֲשֶׁר אָנֹכִי מְצַוְּךָ הַיּוֹם, עַל לְבָבֶךָ.

How many words did you circle? _____

What does the ending ךָ mean? _____

Whom is the prayer addressing? _____

An Ethical Echo

We recite the שְׁמַע and וְאָהַבְתָּ twice a day and put the words in the *mezuzot* on our doorposts and in our tefillin, because that is what the text tells us to do. What may have been meant as a rhetorical flourish (indicating that God's teachings should always be with us, always a part of us), the rabbis transformed into practical acts. And why not? The soul is moved by the actions of the body and the aesthetics of the world around it.

READING PRACTICE

Sometimes the vowel ָ has the sound of the vowel וֹ.

Practice reading the words and phrases below.

1. אָזְנַיִם   קָדְשְׁךָ   כָּל   לְבָבְךָ   בְּכָל

2. הַלֵּילוֹת שֶׁבְּכָל   וּבְכָל נַפְשְׁךָ   וּבְשָׁכְבְּךָ

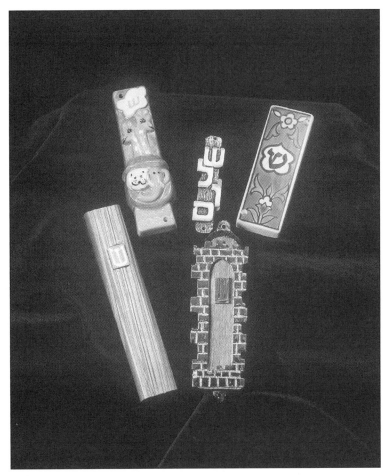

Although *mezuzot* may look different on the outside, inside, each mezuzah contains the same important statement of belief in God.

Back to the Sources

הָ שְׁמַע יִשְׂרָאֵל יְהֹוָה אֱלֹהֵינוּ יְהֹוָה ׀ אֶחָֽד׃ וְאָהַבְתָּ אֵת
יְהֹוָה אֱלֹהֶיךָ בְּכָל־לְבָבְךָ וּבְכָל־נַפְשְׁךָ וּבְכָל־מְאֹדֶֽךָ׃
6 וְהָיוּ הַדְּבָרִים הָאֵלֶּה אֲשֶׁר אָנֹכִי מְצַוְּךָ הַיּוֹם עַל־לְבָבֶֽךָ׃
7 וְשִׁנַּנְתָּם לְבָנֶיךָ וְדִבַּרְתָּ בָּם בְּשִׁבְתְּךָ בְּבֵיתֶךָ וּבְלֶכְתְּךָ
8 בַדֶּרֶךְ וּֽבְשָׁכְבְּךָ וּבְקוּמֶֽךָ׃ וּקְשַׁרְתָּם לְאוֹת עַל־יָדֶךָ וְהָיוּ
9 לְטֹטָפֹת בֵּין עֵינֶֽיךָ׃ וּכְתַבְתָּם עַל־מְזֻזוֹת בֵּיתֶךָ וּבִשְׁעָרֶֽיךָ׃

Above are the verses of the first paragraph of the שְׁמַע (*Deuteronomy 6:4–9*) as they appear in a *tikun*, a printed version of the Torah text. This text not only has all the vowels to help us read, it also indicates the numbers of the verses and the *trope* — the musical notes that tell us how to chant the words. The two asterisks over the ע and the ד in verse 4 draw our attention to their larger size. The two dots at the end of each verse serve as periods.

Below is the same paragraph as it appears in the Torah scroll. This text is uncluttered — no vowels, no *trope*, no punctuation. Note, however, that certain letters have little decorative crowns, called תָּגִים.

שמע ישראל יהוה אלהינו יהוה אחד
ואהבת את יהוה אלהיך בכל לבבך ובכל נפשך
ובכל מאדך והיו הדברים האלה אשר אנכי מצוך
היום על לבבך ושננתם לבניך ודברת בם בשבתך
בביתך ובלכתך בדרך ובשכבך ובקומך וקשרתם
לאות על ידך והיו לטטפת בין עיניך וכתבתם על
מזזות ביתך ובשעריך

More about the Prayer

The שְׁמַע is composed of three paragraphs taken from three different portions of the Torah: Deuteronomy 6:4–9, Deuteronomy 11:13–21, and Numbers 15:37–41.

Many congregations recite out loud only the first paragraph, which we have learned in this chapter, and the last two verses of the last paragraph. These two verses emphasize its three major themes: observing the commandments, being holy, and serving in covenant with God.

PRACTICE:

Read the last two verses of the שְׁמַע.

לְמַעַן תִּזְכְּרוּ — In order that you will remember

וַעֲשִׂיתֶם אֶת כָּל מִצְוֹתָי, — and that you will perform all My mitzvot,

וִהְיִיתֶם קְדֹשִׁים לֵאלֹהֵיכֶם. — and be holy to your God.

אֲנִי יְיָ אֱלֹהֵיכֶם, — I am Adonai your God,

אֲשֶׁר הוֹצֵאתִי אֶתְכֶם — who brought you out

מֵאֶרֶץ מִצְרַיִם, — of the land of Egypt

לִהְיוֹת לָכֶם לֵאלֹהִים, — to be your God.

אֲנִי יְיָ אֱלֹהֵיכֶם. — I am Adonai, your God.

Why do you think the prayer offers a rationale — the liberation from Egypt — for our serving God?

_____

_____

_____

_____

⑨ מִי כָמֹכָה

מִי כָמֹכָה is part of the final blessing recited after the שְׁמַע and just before the עֲמִידָה. Its theme is redemption, both the redemptions of the past and those yet to come. God is characterized here by words reflecting might and salvation — נוֹרָא תְהִלֹּת ("awesome in splendor"), צוּר יִשְׂרָאֵל ("Rock of Israel"), and גְּאָלֵנוּ ("our Redeemer").

The words of this prayer come from the majestic Song at the Sea (EXODUS 15:1–18), sung by the escaping Israelites after the parting of the Red Sea. It resounds with unbridled praise of God, worthy of those who have just been saved from certain death. But its context here is a bit more instrumental. It seeks not just to remind God of past miracles, and our eternal gratitude, but also to encourage God to perform such miracles again, for us, now, on this very day.

PRACTICE:

Read מִי כָמֹכָה.

מִי כָמֹכָה בָּאֵלִם יְיָ,	Who is like You among the gods, Adonai?
מִי כָמֹכָה נֶאְדָּר בַּקֹּדֶשׁ,	Who is like You, majestic in holiness?
נוֹרָא תְהִלֹּת עֹשֵׂה פֶלֶא.	Awesome in splendor, doing wonders?
שִׁירָה חֲדָשָׁה	(With) a new song
שִׁבְּחוּ גְאוּלִים לְשִׁמְךָ	the redeemed people praised Your name
עַל שְׂפַת הַיָּם,	by the shore of the sea.
יַחַד כֻּלָּם הוֹדוּ	Together all of them gave thanks to You
וְהִמְלִיכוּ	and they declared You their Sovereign
וְאָמְרוּ:	and they said:
יְיָ יִמְלֹךְ לְעֹלָם וָעֶד.	May Adonai reign forever and ever.

 continued

PRAYER DICTIONARY

מִי
who

כָּמֹכָה, כְּמֹכָה
like you

בָּאֵלִם
among the gods
[other nations worship]

יְיָ
Adonai

נֶאְדָּר
majestic

בַּקֹּדֶשׁ
in (the) holiness

In the Synagogue

צוּר יִשְׂרָאֵל, — Rock of Israel,

קוּמָה בְּעֶזְרַת יִשְׂרָאֵל, — arise and bring help to Israel,

וּפְדֵה כִנְאֻמֶךָ — and, as You pronounced, redeem

יְהוּדָה וְיִשְׂרָאֵל. — Judah and Israel.

גֹּאֲלֵנוּ — Our Redeemer,

יְיָ צְבָאוֹת שְׁמוֹ, — Adonai of hosts is God's name,

קְדוֹשׁ יִשְׂרָאֵל. — the Holy One of Israel.

בָּרוּךְ אַתָּה יְיָ, — Blessed are You, Adonai,

גָּאַל יִשְׂרָאֵל. — who redeemed Israel.

BUILDING YOUR VOCABULARY

Read each Hebrew word aloud, then connect the Hebrew word to its English translation.

Adonai	מִי
who	נֶאְדָּר
in holiness	יְיָ
majestic	כָּמֹכָה
like You	בַּקֹּדֶשׁ

מִי כָמֹכָה marks the transition between the שְׁמַע and the עֲמִידָה. There is a swelling in the atmosphere, a change of energy, and often a change of tune, as we get ready to stand, and move seamlessly into the next portion of the liturgy. The singing reaches a crescendo with צוּר יִשְׂרָאֵל. But at the end of the blessing, "Blessed are You, Redeemer of Israel," the reader's voice trails off, so the congregation does not hear the words and does not answer אָמֵן.

בַּקֹדֶשׁ

"in (the) holiness"	בַּקֹדֶשׁ is made up of two parts: בַּ means "in the." קֹדֶשׁ means "holiness." Circle the word part that means "in the." בַּקֹדֶשׁ

At the Root

בַּקֹדֶשׁ is built on the root קדשׁ ("holy").

Circle the three root letters in the word בַּקֹדֶשׁ.

Now circle the root letters in each of the following words. Then read them aloud.

קָדוֹשׁ   קָדְשׁוֹ   וְתִתְקַדַּשׁ   הַקָּדוֹשׁ   קִדְּשָׁנוּ

בָּאֵלִם

"among the gods"	בָּאֵלִם is made up of two parts: בָּ means "among the" or "in the." אֵלִם means "gods" — the many false gods that people worshipped. Circle the part of the word that means "among the" or "in the." בָּאֵלִם

The word בָּאֵלִם ("among the gods") is misspelled in the מִי כָמֹכָה.
The י before the ם is missing. The rabbis explain that this misspelling suggests
that the other gods are false gods and do not really exist. The one true God is יְיָ
whose name has two *yuds*.

Back to the Sources

The Torah scribes of old determined that the Song of the Sea should physically reflect the responsive nature of the poem. It is written like an open wall of brickwork, perhaps recalling the way the water walled up on either side of the Israelites when the Red Sea parted. Some say it looks like waves undulating against an unseen barrier. Often, when synagogues and museums display their scrolls, they open them to this portion.

Find and read the first three lines of מִי כָמֹכָה.

אָמַ֥ר 9

אוֹיֵ֛ב אֶרְדֹּ֥ף אַשִּׂ֖יג   אֲחַלֵּ֣ק שָׁלָ֑ל תִּמְלָאֵ֣מוֹ

נַפְשִׁ֔י   אָרִ֣יק חַרְבִּ֔י תּוֹרִישֵׁ֖מוֹ יָדִֽי: נָשַׁ֣פְתָּ י

בְרֽוּחֲךָ֖ כִּסָּ֣מוֹ יָ֑ם   צָֽלֲלוּ֙ כַּֽעוֹפֶ֔רֶת בְּמַ֖יִם

אַדִּירִֽים: מִֽי־כָמֹ֤כָה בָּֽאֵלִם֙ יְהֹוָ֔ה   מִ֤י 11

כָּמֹ֙כָה֙ נֶאְדָּ֣ר בַּקֹּ֔דֶשׁ   נוֹרָ֥א תְהִלֹּ֖ת עֹ֥שֵׂה

פֶ֑לֶא: נָטִ֙יתָ֙ יְמִ֣ינְךָ֔ תִּבְלָעֵ֖מוֹ אָֽרֶץ: נָחִ֥יתָ 12 13

בְחַסְדְּךָ֖ עַם־ז֣וּ גָּאָ֑לְתָּ   נֵהַ֥לְתָּ בְעׇזְּךָ֖ אֶל־נְוֵ֥ה

קׇדְשֶֽׁךָ:   שָֽׁמְע֥וּ עַמִּ֖ים יִרְגָּז֑וּן   חִ֣יל 14

אָחַ֔ז יֹֽשְׁבֵ֖י פְּלָֽשֶׁת: אָ֤ז נִבְהֲלוּ֙ אַלּוּפֵ֣י טו

אֱד֔וֹם   אֵילֵ֣י מוֹאָ֔ב יֹֽאחֲזֵ֖מוֹ רָ֑עַד   נָמֹ֕גוּ

כֹּ֖ל יֹֽשְׁבֵ֥י כְנָֽעַן: 16   תִּפֹּ֨ל עֲלֵיהֶ֤ם אֵימָ֙תָה֙

וָפַ֔חַד   בִּגְדֹ֥ל זְרוֹעֲךָ֖ יִדְּמ֣וּ כָּאָ֑בֶן   עַד־

יַֽעֲבֹ֤ר עַמְּךָ֙ יְהֹוָ֔ה   עַד־יַֽעֲבֹ֖ר עַם־ז֥וּ

קָנִֽיתָ:   תְּבִאֵ֗מוֹ וְתִטָּעֵ֙מוֹ֙ בְּהַ֣ר נַֽחֲלָֽתְךָ֔ 17   מָכ֧וֹן

לְשִׁבְתְּךָ֛ פָּעַ֖לְתָּ יְהֹוָ֑ה   מִקְּדָ֕שׁ אֲדֹנָ֖י כּֽוֹנְנ֥וּ

יָדֶֽיךָ: 18 19   יְהֹוָ֥ה ׀ יִמְלֹ֖ךְ לְעֹלָ֥ם וָעֶֽד:

10 אָבוֹת וְאִמָּהוֹת

The עֲמִידָה is the central prayer of every Jewish service, every day of the year. The rabbis refer to this prayer as, simply, הַתְּפִלָּה ("The Prayer"), indicating its pride of place, and longevity, in the Jewish liturgy. The origins of this prayer are probably found in the Second Temple period shortly before the Common Era.

עֲמִידָה means "standing," for our tradition is to stand during this long prayer. The other common name for it is שְׁמוֹנֶה עֶשְׂרֵה ("eighteen"), for it was originally composed of eighteen blessings, but over eighteen hundred years ago, it adopted an additional blessing, so that now it has nineteen. Even so, the name שְׁמוֹנֶה עֶשְׂרֵה held. We use the term even when referring to this prayer on Shabbat, when, without many of the petitionary prayers, it is reduced to seven blessings.

In every service, the first three and the last three blessings are the same. They praise God and give thanks. The middle blessings change to accommodate the day, be it weekday, Shabbat, or holiday.

אָבוֹת

The עֲמִידָה begins with the אָבוֹת — an establishment of our credentials (we are the children of God's first faithful, Abraham and Sarah), and a panoply of praise. We praise God as awesome, gracious, Creator of all, forgiving, redeeming, loving — a perfect catchall introduction to all the prayers to come.

PRACTICE:

Read the אָבוֹת.

בָּרוּךְ אַתָּה, יְיָ	Blessed are You, Adonai
אֱלֹהֵינוּ וֵאלֹהֵי אֲבוֹתֵינוּ,	our God and God of our fathers,
אֱלֹהֵי אַבְרָהָם, אֱלֹהֵי יִצְחָק,	God of Abraham, God of Isaac,
וֵאלֹהֵי יַעֲקֹב.	and God of Jacob.
הָאֵל הַגָּדוֹל, הַגִּבּוֹר, וְהַנּוֹרָא,	The great, mighty, and awesome God,
אֵל עֶלְיוֹן.	supreme God.
גּוֹמֵל חֲסָדִים טוֹבִים	You do acts of loving-kindness
וְקוֹנֵה הַכֹּל,	and create everything,

 continued

וְזוֹכֵר חַסְדֵי אָבוֹת,	and remember the kindnesses of the fathers,
וּמֵבִיא גוֹאֵל	and You will bring a redeemer
לִבְנֵי בְנֵיהֶם,	to their children's children
לְמַעַן שְׁמוֹ, בְּאַהֲבָה.	for the sake of Your name, and in love.
מֶלֶךְ עוֹזֵר וּמוֹשִׁיעַ וּמָגֵן.	Sovereign, Helper, Rescuer, and Shield.
בָּרוּךְ אַתָּה יְיָ, מָגֵן אַבְרָהָם.	Blessed are You, Adonai, Shield of Abraham.

אָבוֹת וְאִמָּהוֹת

In the late twentieth century, as women achieved greater prominence in synagogue ritual, Jewish communities sought to give women greater prominence in the prayer book as well. Up until then, liturgical references clustered around a handful of patriarchs: Abraham, Isaac, Jacob, Moses, David. Increasingly, prayer books include the matriarchs — Sarah, Rebecca, Leah, and Rachel — in the first paragraph of the עֲמִידָה.

PRACTICE:

Read the אָבוֹת וְאִמָּהוֹת.

בָּרוּךְ אַתָּה, יְיָ	Blessed are You, Adonai
אֱלֹהֵינוּ וֵאלֹהֵי	our God and God of
אֲבוֹתֵינוּ וְאִמּוֹתֵינוּ,	our fathers and mothers,
אֱלֹהֵי אַבְרָהָם, אֱלֹהֵי יִצְחָק,	God of Abraham, God of Isaac,
וֵאלֹהֵי יַעֲקֹב,	and God of Jacob,
אֱלֹהֵי שָׂרָה, אֱלֹהֵי רִבְקָה,	God of Sarah, God of Rebecca,
אֱלֹהֵי לֵאָה, וֵאלֹהֵי רָחֵל.	God of Leah, and God of Rachel.
הָאֵל הַגָּדוֹל, הַגִּבּוֹר, וְהַנּוֹרָא,	The great, mighty, and awesome God,
אֵל עֶלְיוֹן.	supreme God.
גּוֹמֵל חֲסָדִים טוֹבִים	You do acts of loving-kindness
וְקוֹנֵה הַכֹּל, וְזוֹכֵר	and create everything, and remember
חַסְדֵי אָבוֹת וְאִמָּהוֹת,	the kindnesses of the fathers and mothers,
וּמֵבִיא גוֹאֵל/גְּאֻלָּה	and You will bring a redeemer/redemption
לִבְנֵי בְנֵיהֶם,	to their children's children
לְמַעַן שְׁמוֹ, בְּאַהֲבָה.	for the sake of Your name, and in love.
מֶלֶךְ עוֹזֵר וּמוֹשִׁיעַ וּמָגֵן.	Sovereign, Helper, Rescuer, and Shield.
בָּרוּךְ אַתָּה יְיָ,	Blessed are You, Adonai,
מָגֵן אַבְרָהָם וְעֶזְרַת שָׂרָה.	Shield of Abraham and Help of Sarah.

Prayer Variations

For millennia, many Jews have professed a belief in a messiah, גּוֹאֵל — a redeemer — a human being of flesh and blood who would usher in the messianic world. Stories from the Holocaust tell us that Jews went to their deaths singing: "I believe, with complete faith, in the coming of the messiah." Some of us set aside a chair for Elijah, the escort of the Messiah, at the *brit milah* ceremony *(bris)* and some welcome Elijah at a seder with Elijah's cup (of wine), opening the door for him and singing songs urging him to come soon.

Others believe that while one day we will witness גְּאֻלָּה — a messianic era — it will be achieved by our own hard work, and not by a Messiah. It is as if a small piece of the Messiah is already within each of us, waiting to be revealed.

Think About It!

In the אָבוֹת, God is described as both our God, and as the God of Abraham, the God of Isaac, the God of Jacob; the God of Sarah, the God of Rebecca, the God of Leah, and the God of Rachel — a God both communal and personal. While God is the God of all of us, God is also the God of each of us. We each travel our own path to God and forge our own relationship with our God.

PRAYER DICTIONARY

אָבוֹת	fathers
אֲבוֹתֵינוּ	our fathers
אֱלֹהֵי	God of
אַבְרָהָם	Abraham
יִצְחָק	Isaac
יַעֲקֹב	Jacob

BUILDING YOUR VOCABULARY

Circle the Hebrew words that correspond to the English.

fathers	אַבְרָהָם	אָבוֹת	אוֹר
our fathers	אֲבוֹתֵינוּ	אֱלֹהֵינוּ	אַתָּה
God of	יִשְׂרָאֵל	וְאָהַבְתָּ	אֱלֹהֵי

WHAT'S IN A NAME?

Connect the Hebrew and English names of the fathers.

Isaac   אַבְרָהָם

Jacob   יִצְחָק

Abraham   יַעֲקֹב

BUILDING YOUR VOCABULARY

Circle the Hebrew words that correspond to the English.

mothers	הָאֲדָמָה	אִמָּהוֹת	אֱמֶת
our mothers	הָאָרֶץ	אֵלִיָּהוּ	אִמּוֹתֵינוּ
God of	אֱלֹהֵי	אַבְרָהָם	אָרוֹן

WHAT'S IN A NAME?

Connect the Hebrew and English names of the mothers.

Leah   שָׂרָה

Sarah   רִבְקָה

Rachel   לֵאָה

Rebecca   רָחֵל

BUILDING YOUR VOCABULARY

The אָבוֹת lists four words to describe God's greatness.
Write the English meaning for each one.

_____	_____
הַגִּבּוֹר	הַגָּדוֹל
_____	_____
עֶלְיוֹן	וְהַנּוֹרָא

In the אָבוֹת we see four roles that God plays in the lives
of the Jewish people.
Write the English meaning for each one.

_____	_____
עוֹזֵר	מֶלֶךְ
_____	_____
וּמָגֵן	וּמוֹשִׁיעַ

Think About It!

There are many instances in Jewish liturgy where adjectives praising God are heaped one on the other. Why do you think a single word of praise was insufficient for the rabbis who wrote the liturgy?

_____

_____

_____

_____

_____

PRAYER DICTIONARY

הַגָּדוֹל
the great

הַגִּבּוֹר
the mighty

וְהַנּוֹרָא
and the awesome

עֶלְיוֹן
supreme

חֲסָדִים טוֹבִים
acts of loving-kindness

מֶלֶךְ
sovereign

עוֹזֵר
helper

וּמוֹשִׁיעַ
and rescuer

וּמָגֵן
and shield

הַגָּדוֹל, הַגִּבּוֹר, וְהַנּוֹרָא

"the great, the mighty, and the awesome"	הַגָּדוֹל means "the great."
	הַגִּבּוֹר means "the mighty."
	וְהַנּוֹרָא means "the awesome."
	The prefixes וְ and הַ mean "and" and "the" respectively.
	Circle the prefixes in the words above.

Torah Connection

Read the following verse from Deuteronomy 10:17.

כִּי יְיָ אֱלֹהֵיכֶם הוּא אֱלֹהֵי הָאֱלֹהִים
וַאֲדֹנֵי הָאֲדֹנִים הָאֵל הַגָּדֹל הַגִּבֹּר וְהַנּוֹרָא

Do you recognize the underlined words?

Write their English meaning.

_____

_____

Why do you think the words הָאֵל הַגָּדֹל הַגִּבֹּר וְהַנּוֹרָא are written in the Torah and repeated in the עֲמִידָה?

_____

_____

_____

עֶלְיוֹן

"supreme," "highest"

God is called "supreme" or "highest."

עַל means "on" or "above."

Being called to the Torah is known as an עֲלִיָּה ("going up"). Yet the rabbis taught that the Torah is not in heaven, but rather is here on earth. It is for people to interpret, learn from, and use as a guide to living. How, then, would you explain the term עֲלִיָּה?

_____

_____

חֲסָדִים טוֹבִים

"acts of loving-kindness"

חֲסָדִים means "acts of loving-kindness."

טוֹבִים means "good."

Do you think the adjective טוֹבִים is redundant? Are acts of loving-kindness always "good"?

Explain your anwer.

_____

_____

Young people can show love and respect for their parents and grandparents by helping with chores around the house.

מֶלֶךְ עוֹזֵר וּמוֹשִׁיעַ וּמָגֵן

"sovereign,
helper,
and rescuer,
and shield"

מֶלֶךְ means "king" or "sovereign."

עוֹזֵר means "helper."

וּמוֹשִׁיעַ means "and rescuer."

וּמָגֵן means "and shield."

Circle the prefix that means "and" in these two words: וּמוֹשִׁיעַ וּמָגֵן

מֶלֶךְ עוֹזֵר וּמוֹשִׁיעַ וּמָגֵן.

בָּרוּךְ אַתָּה יְיָ, מָגֵן אַבְרָהָם.

Circle the Hebrew word for "shield" in each line above.

Approaching God

When we recite the עֲמִידָה, it is as if we are granted an audience before God. As we begin, the traditional practice is to take three steps forward, as though approaching the divine throne, and then to stand with our feet planted firmly together. We bend our knees when we say בָּרוּךְ at the beginning of the אָבוֹת, bow when we say אַתָּה, and stand erect at יְיָ. We bow again when we say the last line of the blessing.

Likewise, at the end of the עֲמִידָה, the traditional practice is to take three steps back, bow to the left, right, and center, then take our leave.

In most American synagogues, when we face the Ark, we face east, toward Jerusalem, the place where the Temple stood.

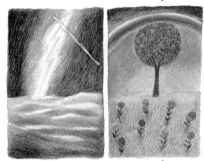

גְּבוּרוֹת 11

The second blessing of the Amidah, גְּבוּרוֹת ("powers"), expresses the belief in God's power to grant us health, freedom, strength, and everlasting life.

PRACTICE:

Read the גְּבוּרוֹת.

אַתָּה גִבּוֹר לְעוֹלָם, אֲדֹנָי,
You are eternally mighty (powerful), Adonai,

מְחַיֵּה הַכֹּל/מֵתִים אַתָּה,
You give life to all/the dead,

רַב לְהוֹשִׁיעַ.
great is Your power to save.

מְכַלְכֵּל חַיִּים בְּחֶסֶד,
With kindness You sustain the living,

מְחַיֵּה הַכֹּל/מֵתִים
give life to all/the dead

בְּרַחֲמִים רַבִּים.
with great compassion (mercy).

סוֹמֵךְ נוֹפְלִים, וְרוֹפֵא חוֹלִים,
You help the failing, and heal the sick,

וּמַתִּיר אֲסוּרִים, וּמְקַיֵּם
and You free the captive, and keep

אֱמוּנָתוֹ לִישֵׁנֵי עָפָר.
faith with those who sleep in the dust.

מִי כָמוֹךָ, בַּעַל גְּבוּרוֹת,
Who is like You, God of Power,

וּמִי דוֹמֶה לָּךְ,
and who is comparable to You,

מֶלֶךְ מֵמִית וּמְחַיֵּה
Sovereign who brings death and gives life

וּמַצְמִיחַ יְשׁוּעָה?
and who is a source of salvation?

וְנֶאֱמָן אַתָּה לְהַחֲיוֹת
You are faithful to give life

הַכֹּל/מֵתִים.
to all/the dead.

בָּרוּךְ אַתָּה יְיָ,
Blessed are You, Adonai,

מְחַיֵּה הַכֹּל/הַמֵּתִים.
who gives life to all/the dead.

Think About It!

Reform and Reconstructionist worshippers, who use the phrases מְחַיֵּה הַכֹּל and מְחַיֵּה כָּל חַי ("gives life to everything") instead of מְחַיֵּה הַמֵּתִים ("revives the dead"), state a belief in the majesterial goodness of God but recast the sentiment away from resurrection. Instead, they express the belief that God revives the spirit of the downtrodden, the broken, the weak, and the lost, and sustains us in this life, which is miracle enough.

Which version of the גְּבוּרוֹת is found in your synagogue's prayer book?

PRAYER DICTIONARY

אַתָּה
you (are)

גִּבּוֹר
mighty, powerful

לְעוֹלָם
eternally

מְחַיֶּה
give life

לְהוֹשִׁיעַ
to save

חַיִּים
life, the living

בְּרַחֲמִים
with compassion, mercy

מִי כָמוֹךָ
who is like you?

POWERFUL WORDS

Circle the Hebrew word or phrase that corresponds to the English.

who is like you?	מִי כָמוֹךָ	חֲסָדִים טוֹבִים	לְעוֹלָם וָעֶד
life, the living	אֱמֶת	זִכָּרוֹן	חַיִּים
eternally	עֶלְיוֹן	לְעוֹלָם	וְעַל
mighty, powerful	גִּבּוֹר	גּוֹמֵל	מֶלֶךְ
you (are)	אֶחָד	אַתָּה	אָבוֹת
give life	מְחַיֶּה	מָגֵן	מוֹשִׁיעַ
with compassion, mercy	וּבְרָצוֹן	בְּרַחֲמִים	בְּאַהֲבָה
to save	לְהוֹשִׁיעַ	לִיצִיאַת	לְהַדְלִיק

Prayer Themes

In the first blessing of the עֲמִידָה — the אָבוֹת — we speak in generalities about God's goodness. In the second blessing — the גְּבוּרוֹת — our words about God's mercy and kindness are more specific. Interestingly, most of these acts we, too, can perform. We can help encourage the disheartened, raise the fallen, feed the hungry, heal the sick, free the oppressed. And in doing so, we might help give renewed life to those in need.

We can feel God's presence through our own acts of kindness. By donating this ambulance to the State of Israel, the Jewish communities of France helped give renewed life to those in need.

אַתָּה גִּבּוֹר לְעוֹלָם

"you are eternally mighty (powerful)"

Underline the pronoun that addresses God in the phrase אַתָּה גִּבּוֹר לְעוֹלָם. גִּבּוֹר means "mighty" or "powerful."

Can you see the connection between גִּבּוֹר and the name of the blessing you are studying — גְּבוּרוֹת?

מְחַיֶּה

"give life"

The words מְחַיֶּה and חַיִּים are related. They share the Hebrew root חיה ("live"). (Perhaps you have clinked glasses, made a toast, and wished someone לְחַיִּים. Or even sung the song, "To life, to life, לְחַיִּים!")

You may also have given — or received — a gift of money in multiples of eighteen in honor of a wedding or bar or bat mitzvah. In Hebrew, there is a system — called *gematria* — in which each letter has a numerical value and words can be interpreted by adding up the value of their letters. The numerical number of חַי is determined by adding the value of the eighth letter, ח (eight), to the value of the tenth letter, י (ten), bringing the total to eighteen. Eighteen, therefore, symbolizes life.

מְכַלְכֵּל חַיִּים בְּחֶסֶד

"with kindness you sustain the living"

Circle the word that means "living" or "life."
Underline the word that means "kindness."

מְכַלְכֵּל חַיִּים בְּחֶסֶד

בְּרַחֲמִים רַבִּים

"with great compassion"

Underline the word that means "with compassion" or "with mercy."

בְּרַחֲמִים רַבִּים

The root of בְּרַחֲמִים is רחם.

The root רחם tells us that "compassion" or "mercy" is part of the word's meaning. God is sometimes referred to as אֵל מָלֵא רַחֲמִים.

This means "God full of _____."

Below are three other names by which God is known. Circle the root letters רחם in each phrase.

אֵל חַנּוּן וְרַחוּם   אַב הָרַחֲמִים   הָרַחֲמָן

Merciful Parent   Gracious and Compassionate God   The Merciful One

What do these names have in common?

_____

Why do you think that there are so many names for God in the Jewish tradition?

_____

מִי כָמוֹךָ

"who is like you?"

מִי means _____.

כָמוֹךָ means _____.

כְּמוֹ means "like."

ךָ at the end of a word means _____.

Circle כָמוֹךָ or כָמֹכָה in each line below. Then read each line.

1. אֵין כָּמוֹךָ בָאֱלֹהִים, אֲדֹנָי, וְאֵין כְּמַעֲשֶׂיךָ.

2. מִי כָמֹכָה בָּאֵלִם, יְיָ?

3. מִי כָמֹכָה, נֶאְדָּר בַּקֹּדֶשׁ.

קְדוּשָׁה 12

The first three blessings in the עֲמִידָה speak of three different ways we know God: through membership in the Jewish people (אָבוֹת), through daily miracles (גְבוּרוֹת), and now, through the mystery of holiness (קְדוּשָׁה).

When the עֲמִידָה is recited in a minyan — the group of ten adults traditionally required for a prayer service — the קְדוּשָׁה is said out loud and responsively. In the Shabbat morning version, the word קָדוֹשׁ ("holy"), or a form of it, occurs no less than eight times.

When reciting this prayer, it is as if we are trying to be transported to the heavenly realm and join with the entourage of angels in Isaiah's vision, who constantly praise God saying: קָדוֹשׁ, קָדוֹשׁ, קָדוֹשׁ ("Holy, holy, holy") (ISAIAH 6:3). We rise up on our toes three times as we recite these words, thus elevating ourselves in the way the angels are elevated in God's eyes.

PRACTICE:

Read the קְדוּשָׁה.

נְקַדֵּשׁ אֶת שִׁמְךָ בָּעוֹלָם,	Let us sanctify Your name in the world,
כְּשֵׁם שֶׁמַּקְדִּישִׁים	as they sanctify
אוֹתוֹ בִּשְׁמֵי מָרוֹם,	it in the highest heavens,
כַּכָּתוּב עַל יַד נְבִיאֶךָ,	as it is written by Your prophet,
וְקָרָא זֶה אֶל זֶה וְאָמַר:	and one called to another and said:
קָדוֹשׁ קָדוֹשׁ קָדוֹשׁ	"Holy, Holy, Holy
יְיָ צְבָאוֹת,	is Adonai of the heavenly legions,
מְלֹא כָל הָאָרֶץ כְּבוֹדוֹ.	the whole earth is full of God's glory."
בָּרוּךְ כְּבוֹד יְיָ	Blessed is the glory of God
מִמְּקוֹמוֹ.	from God's place.
יִמְלֹךְ יְיָ לְעוֹלָם,	Adonai will rule forever;
אֱלֹהַיִךְ צִיּוֹן,	your God, O Zion,
לְדֹר וָדֹר, הַלְלוּיָהּ.	from generation to generation. Halleluyah!

⬅ *continued*

PRAYER DICTIONARY

נְקַדֵּשׁ
let us sanctify

שִׁמְךָ
your name

כְּבוֹדוֹ
God's glory

יִמְלֹךְ
will rule

לְדוֹר וָדוֹר
from generation to generation

נַגִּיד
we will tell

גָּדְלֶךָ
your greatness

לְדוֹר וָדוֹר	From generation to generation
נַגִּיד גָּדְלֶךָ,	we will tell of Your greatness,
וּלְנֵצַח נְצָחִים	and for all eternity
קְדֻשָּׁתְךָ נַקְדִּישׁ.	we will proclaim Your holiness.
וְשִׁבְחֲךָ אֱלֹהֵינוּ	And our praise of You, O God,
מִפִּינוּ לֹא יָמוּשׁ	will not depart from our mouths
לְעוֹלָם וָעֶד.	forever and ever.
בָּרוּךְ אַתָּה יְיָ, הָאֵל הַקָּדוֹשׁ.	Blessed are You, Adonai, the holy God.

BUILDING YOUR VOCABULARY

On the right are words from the קְדוּשָׁה. On the left are words you already know. Draw lines to connect the related words. (Hint: Look for common roots.) Then write the English meaning of the Hebrew word from the קְדוּשָׁה on the line next to the number.

הַגָּדוֹל	נְקַדֵּשׁ	1.	_____
הַגָּדָה	יִמְלֹךְ	2.	_____
כָּבוֹד	גָּדְלֶךָ	3.	_____
מֶלֶךְ	שִׁמְךָ	4.	_____
קָדוֹשׁ	כְּבוֹדוֹ	5.	_____
שֵׁם	נַגִּיד	6.	_____

Holding a baby can fill us with the wonder of God's creations and all the possibilities that the future can bring.

From the Sources

The core of the קְדוּשָׁה consists of three biblical verses:

קָדוֹשׁ קָדוֹשׁ קָדוֹשׁ   "Holy, Holy, Holy

יְיָ צְבָאוֹת,   is Adonai of the heavenly legions,

מְלֹא כָל הָאָרֶץ כְּבוֹדוֹ.   the whole earth is full of God's glory."

— *Isaiah 6:3*

בָּרוּךְ כְּבוֹד יְיָ   Blessed is the glory of Adonai

מִמְּקוֹמוֹ.   from God's place.

— *Ezekiel 3:12*

יִמְלֹךְ יְיָ לְעוֹלָם,   Adonai will rule forever,

אֱלֹהַיִךְ צִיּוֹן   your God, O Zion,

לְדֹר וָדֹר, הַלְלוּיָהּ.   from generation to generation. Halleluyah!

— *Psalms 146:10*

It is in the first of these verses that the prophet Isaiah describes the beautiful and mystical vision of God sitting on the Divine Throne surrounded by angels.

How can we understand holiness? Perhaps we can best imagine it as life's fourth dimension, that invisible plane of existence that turns Friday night into Shabbat, a simple act into a mitzvah, and a wish into a prayer.

Give your own interpretation of holiness.

_____

_____

_____

Prayer Building Blocks

נְקַדֵּשׁ אֶת שִׁמְךָ בָּעוֹלָם

"let us sanctify your name in the world"

נְקַדֵּשׁ means "let us sanctify."

נְקַדֵּשׁ is built on the root קדשׁ.

Words built on the root קדשׁ have "_____" as part of their meaning.

שִׁמְךָ means "your name."

שֵׁם means _____.

ךָ means _____.

Whose name are we sanctifying? _____

בָּעוֹלָם means "in the world."

בָּ means _____.

עוֹלָם means _____.

Circle all the words with the root קדשׁ in the קְדוּשָׁה on pages 66–67.

מְלֹא כָל הָאָרֶץ כְּבוֹדוֹ

"the whole earth is full of God's glory"

Underline הָאָרֶץ ("the earth") in the following sentence from the Torah. We read that God created the heavens and the earth in six days and on the seventh day God rested.

כִּי שֵׁשֶׁת יָמִים עָשָׂה יְיָ אֶת הַשָּׁמַיִם וְאֶת הָאָרֶץ,
וּבַיּוֹם הַשְּׁבִיעִי שָׁבַת וַיִּנָּפַשׁ.

What is the name of the seventh day, on which God rested? Circle a variation of the word in the lines above.

כְּבוֹדוֹ means "his glory."

וֹ means "his" but, since God is neither male nor female, in this book we translate כְּבוֹדוֹ as "God's glory."

יִמְלֹךְ יְיָ לְעוֹלָם

"Adonai will rule forever"	יִמְלֹךְ means "will rule."

The root of יִמְלֹךְ is מלכ.

Words built on the root מלכ have "_____" as part of their meaning.

י at the beginning of a verb often indicates the future tense.

לְדוֹר וָדוֹר נַגִּיד גָּדְלֶךָ

"from generation to generation we will tell of your greatness"

דוֹר means "generation."

לְדוֹר וָדוֹר is a phrase meaning "from generation to generation."

Explain in your own words the phrase "from generation to generation."

_____

Read this sentence from the Haggadah. Circle the Hebrew phrase that means "in every generation."

בְּכָל דוֹר וָדוֹר חַיָּב אָדָם   In every generation, each of us

לִרְאוֹת אֶת עַצְמוֹ   should feel as though we ourselves

כְּאִלּוּ הוּא יָצָא מִמִּצְרַיִם.   had gone forth from Egypt.

נַגִּיד means "we will tell" or "we will relate."

You know the word הַגָּדָה. Can you see the connection between נַגִּיד and הַגָּדָה?

On which holiday do we use a הַגָּדָה? _____

הַגָּדָה means "telling" or "relating." What do we tell or relate on this holiday?

_____

גָּדְלֶךָ means "your greatness."

גָּדוֹל is the Hebrew word for "great" or "big."

What does the ending ךָ mean? _____

קְדוּשַׁת הַיּוֹם

On Shabbat, instead of the middle thirteen עֲמִידָה blessings for weekdays, we have one: the blessing for the Sabbath day. This yields a total of seven blessings, corresponding to the seven days of the week.

More than asking for gifts such as health, redemption, justice, bounty, or even peace, as the weekday prayers do, this prayer asks for mutual fulfillment. May God be happy with our rest, it says, and may we become sated with God's goodness.

PRACTICE:

Read קְדוּשַׁת הַיּוֹם.

אֱלֹהֵינוּ וֵאלֹהֵי	Our God and God of
אֲבוֹתֵינוּ וְאִמּוֹתֵינוּ,	our fathers and mothers,
רְצֵה בִמְנוּחָתֵנוּ.	take pleasure in our rest.
קַדְּשֵׁנוּ בְּמִצְוֹתֶיךָ	Make us holy through Your commandments
וְתֵן חֶלְקֵנוּ בְּתוֹרָתֶךָ,	and let Your Torah be our portion.
שַׂבְּעֵנוּ מִטּוּבֶךָ	Satisfy us from Your abundance
וְשַׂמְּחֵנוּ בִּישׁוּעָתֶךָ.	and make us happy in Your salvation.
וְטַהֵר לִבֵּנוּ	Purify our heart
לְעָבְדְּךָ בֶּאֱמֶת.	so that we may serve You with truth.
וְהַנְחִילֵנוּ, יְיָ אֱלֹהֵינוּ	Bequeath to us, Adonai our God,
בְּאַהֲבָה וּבְרָצוֹן	in love and willingly
שַׁבַּת קָדְשֶׁךָ,	Your holy Sabbath,
וְיָנוּחוּ בָה יִשְׂרָאֵל	then will Israel who sanctifies Your name rest on it
מְקַדְּשֵׁי שְׁמֶךָ.	(the Sabbath day).
בָּרוּךְ אַתָּה יְיָ,	Blessed are You, Adonai,
מְקַדֵּשׁ הַשַּׁבָּת.	who sanctifies the Sabbath.

הוֹדָאָה 13

The עֲמִידָה is coming to a close. How does one end such a litany of prayers? The rabbis of old — as if fearful of leaving something out — fashioned this comprehensive prayer of thanksgiving. Its generalities contribute to its power. For each of us carries our own bundle of gratitude. The liturgical template shared here — thanking God for our lives, our souls, and the miracles with which we are blessed daily — invites the private acknowledging of our thanks before God.

PRACTICE:

Read the הוֹדָאָה.

מוֹדִים אֲנַחְנוּ לָךְ,	We give thanks to You,
שָׁאַתָּה הוּא יְיָ אֱלֹהֵינוּ	for You are Adonai our God
וֵאלֹהֵי אֲבוֹתֵינוּ וְאִמּוֹתֵינוּ	and the God of our fathers and mothers
לְעוֹלָם וָעֶד.	forever and ever.
צוּר חַיֵּינוּ,	You are the Rock of our lives,
מָגֵן יִשְׁעֵנוּ,	and the Shield who saves us,
אַתָּה הוּא לְדוֹר וָדוֹר.	from generation to generation.
נוֹדֶה לְךָ	We will give thanks to You
וּנְסַפֵּר תְּהִלָּתֶךָ,	and tell Your praises,
עַל חַיֵּינוּ	on account of our lives
הַמְּסוּרִים בְּיָדֶךָ,	that we submit to You,
וְעַל נִשְׁמוֹתֵינוּ	and for our souls
הַפְּקוּדוֹת לָךְ,	that are entrusted to You,
וְעַל נִסֶּיךָ	and for Your miracles
שֶׁבְּכָל יוֹם עִמָּנוּ,	that are with us every day,
וְעַל נִפְלְאוֹתֶיךָ	and for Your wonders
וְטוֹבוֹתֶיךָ שֶׁבְּכָל עֵת,	and the good (that exist) at all times,
עֶרֶב וָבֹקֶר וְצָהֳרָיִם.	evening and morning and noon.

 continued

73

הַטוֹב O You, who are good

כִּי לֹא כָלוּ רַחֲמֶיךָ, and whose mercies are never exhausted,

וְהַמְרַחֵם, and merciful being,

כִּי לֹא תַמּוּ חֲסָדֶיךָ, whose loving-kindness never ends,

מֵעוֹלָם קִוִּינוּ לָךְ. we have always placed our hope in You.

וְעַל כֻּלָּם And for all this

יִתְבָּרַךְ וְיִתְרוֹמַם שִׁמְךָ, Your name will be blessed and exalted,

מַלְכֵּנוּ, תָּמִיד לְעוֹלָם וָעֶד. our Sovereign, always and forever.

וְכֹל הַחַיִּים יוֹדוּךָ סֶּלָה, And all living things will acknowledge

וִיהַלְלוּ אֶת שִׁמְךָ בֶּאֱמֶת, and praise Your name in truth,

הָאֵל יְשׁוּעָתֵנוּ the God who is our Rescuer

וְעֶזְרָתֵנוּ סֶלָה. and our Helper.

בָּרוּךְ אַתָּה יְיָ, Blessed are You, Adonai,

הַטוֹב שִׁמְךָ whose name is good

וּלְךָ נָאֶה לְהוֹדוֹת. and to whom thanks is due.

The מוֹדָה אֲנִי prayer, said first thing upon awakening in the morning, thanks God for returning our souls to us and for giving us a brand new day.

BUILDING YOUR VOCABULARY

Three words in the Prayer Dictionary are related to "thanks." Read them aloud and write their English meaning below.

מוֹדִים _____

לְהוֹדוֹת _____

נוֹדֶה _____

Two words in the Prayer Dictionary are related to "praise." Read them aloud and write their English meaning below.

תְּהִלָּתֶךְ _____

וִיהַלְלוּ _____

Think About It!

הוֹדָאָה can mean both "acknowledgment" and "thanks." The phrase מוֹדִים אֲנַחְנוּ לָךְ can mean (1) we thank You, God or (2) we acknowledge You, God.

In your opinion, are thanking and acknowledging the same thing? Can you do one without the other? Explain your answer.

_____

_____

_____

_____

PRAYER DICTIONARY

מוֹדִים
thank, give thanks

אֲנַחְנוּ
we

נוֹדֶה
we will thank, give thanks

תְּהִלָּתֶךְ
your praises

וִיהַלְלוּ
(they) will praise

שִׁמְךָ
your name

בֶּאֱמֶת
in truth

לְהוֹדוֹת
to thank

מוֹדִים אֲנַחְנוּ לָךְ

"we give thanks to you"

מוֹדִים means "thank" or "give thanks."

Practice reading this line from the prayer said upon waking in the morning.

A male says: מוֹדֶה אֲנִי לְפָנֶיךָ, מֶלֶךְ חַי וְקַיָּם

A female says: מוֹדָה אֲנִי לְפָנֶיךָ, מֶלֶךְ חַי וְקַיָּם

Circle the words in the lines above that mean "thank."

Notice that the form of the verb is different for a male and female.

נוֹדֶה לְךָ

"we will give thanks to you"

נוֹדֶה means "we will give thanks."

לְךָ means "to you."

לְ means "to."

ךָ means _____.

Perhaps you've heard someone say תּוֹדָה רַבָּה or תּוֹדָה, meaning "thank you" or "thank you very much." מוֹדִים, תּוֹדָה, נוֹדֶה, and all share the same root letters, ידה.

וּנְסַפֵּר תְּהִלָּתֶךָ

"and we will tell of your praises"

תְּהִלָּתֶךָ means "your praises."

The root of תְּהִלָּתֶךָ is הלל.

The root הלל tells us that "praise" is part of a word's meaning.

וִיהַלְלוּ אֶת שִׁמְךָ בֶּאֱמֶת

"and we will praise your name in truth"

וִיהַלְלוּ means "and will praise."

The root of וִיהַלְלוּ is הלל.

Words built on the root הלל have "_____" as part of their meaning.

שִׁמְךָ means "your name."

שֵׁם means _____.

ךָ is a suffix meaning _____.

To whose name are we referring? _____.

בֶּאֱמֶת means "in truth."

Circle the word part that means "in."

אֱמֶת means _____.

Why do you think it is necessary to add the words "in truth" to the phrase "and will praise your name"?

_____

_____

In the Synagogue

Traditional practice is to bow from the waist, without bending the knee, at the beginning and at the end of this blessing.

Saying Thank You

In the הוֹדָאָה prayer you have learned different Hebrew forms of the word "thank."

Read each prayer sentence below and circle the word(s) that mean(s) "thank."

1. מוֹדִים אֲנַחְנוּ לָךְ, שָׁאַתָּה הוּא יְיָ אֱלֹהֵינוּ.

2. נוֹדֶה לֵאלֹהֵינוּ. נוֹדֶה לַאדוֹנֵנוּ. נוֹדֶה לְמַלְכֵּנוּ. נוֹדֶה לְמוֹשִׁיעֵנוּ.

3. בָּרוּךְ אַתָּה, יְיָ, הַטּוֹב שִׁמְךָ וּלְךָ נָאֶה לְהוֹדוֹת.

4. וַאֲנַחְנוּ כּוֹרְעִים וּמִשְׁתַּחֲוִים וּמוֹדִים לִפְנֵי מֶלֶךְ מַלְכֵי הַמְּלָכִים, הַקָּדוֹשׁ בָּרוּךְ הוּא.

5. טוֹב לְהוֹדוֹת לַייָ וּלְזַמֵּר לְשִׁמְךָ עֶלְיוֹן.

6. מוֹדָה אֲנִי לְפָנֶיךָ מֶלֶךְ חַי וְקַיָּם.

7. נוֹדֶה לְךָ וּנְסַפֵּר תְּהִלָּתֶךָ.

8. וְעַל הַכֹּל יְיָ אֱלֹהֵינוּ, אֲנַחְנוּ מוֹדִים לָךְ, וּמְבָרְכִים אוֹתָךְ.

Which of the lines above appear in the הוֹדָאָה?

Write the numbers: #_____   #_____   #_____

Public acknowledgment and thanks for a job well done make teacher *and* student feel good.

בִּרְכַּת שָׁלוֹם ⬠14

שָׁלוֹם רָב

The עֲמִידָה ends with a call for peace, as does the Kaddish, the evening Sh'ma, Birkat Hamazon, and the Priestly Blessing. So central to Jewish thought is peace that שָׁלוֹם is used as one of God's names. שָׁלוֹם is also the way we greet people and the way we take our leave of them. The ancient rabbis consciously structured the עֲמִידָה so that of all the blessings, this one — בִּרְכַּת שָׁלוֹם ("prayer for peace") — would come last.

שָׁלוֹם bears within it the meanings of wholeness, of completeness, of fullness. It is as if we say that peace is not a state we can pursue in and of itself, but derives from tending to other goals. When there is no want, no fear, no strife — and when things are whole — with no losses, no pains, no gaps, no hatred, that is when we will know true peace.

There are two versions of בִּרְכַּת שָׁלוֹם. The first, שָׁלוֹם רָב ("abundant peace"), is recited in the afternoon and evening services. The second, שִׂים שָׁלוֹם ("grant peace"), is recited in the morning service.

PRACTICE:

Read שָׁלוֹם רָב.

שָׁלוֹם רָב	May You grant great peace
עַל יִשְׂרָאֵל עַמְּךָ תָּשִׂים לְעוֹלָם,	upon Israel Your people forever,
כִּי אַתָּה הוּא מֶלֶךְ	for You are the Sovereign
אָדוֹן לְכָל הַשָּׁלוֹם.	of all peace.
וְטוֹב בְּעֵינֶיךָ	And may it be good in Your eyes
לְבָרֵךְ אֶת עַמְּךָ יִשְׂרָאֵל	to bless Your people Israel
(וְאֶת כָּל הָעַמִּים)	(and all peoples)
בְּכָל עֵת וּבְכָל שָׁעָה	at every time and every hour
בִּשְׁלוֹמֶךָ.	with Your peace.
בָּרוּךְ אַתָּה יְיָ,	Blessed are You, Adonai,
הַמְבָרֵךְ אֶת עַמּוֹ יִשְׂרָאֵל	who blesses God's people Israel
בַּשָּׁלוֹם.	with peace.

PRAYER DICTIONARY

שָׁלוֹם
peace

רָב
great

יִשְׂרָאֵל
Israel

עַמְּךָ
your people

וְטוֹב
and may it be good

בְּעֵינֶיךָ
in your eyes

לְבָרֵךְ
to bless

בִּשְׁלוֹמֶךָ
with your peace

BUILDING YOUR VOCABULARY

Many of the words in שָׁלוֹם רָב are commonly found in Jewish liturgy.

Read through the words in the Prayer Dictionary. Are any familiar to you?

Complete the following Prayer Dictionary activities.

1. Circle the two words that share common root letters and meaning.

2. Three words in this list share the common ending ךָ ("you" or "your"). Write the English meaning of each word next to the Hebrew.

עַמְּךָ _____

בְּעֵינֶיךָ _____

בִּשְׁלוֹמֶךָ _____

In the Hebrew words above, circle the prefix that means "with" or "in."

Think About It!

In this, and in other versions of the prayer, the words וְאֵת כָּל הָעַמִּים ("and all peoples") are inserted, for there is no such thing as partial peace. So even as we pray for peace for the people Israel, so do we pray for peace for all the world.

A peaceful family life can help add peace to the world.

Prayer Building Blocks

שָׁלוֹם רָב עַל יִשְׂרָאֵל

"great peace upon Israel"	שָׁלוֹם רָב means "great peace." The root of שָׁלוֹם — שלמ — indicates that "peace," "harmony," "completeness," or "wholeness" is part of a word's meaning. What do you think the connection is between the different meanings of שלמ, including "hello" and "good-bye"? _____ _____ Circle the three root letters in בִּשְׁלוֹמֶךְ ("with your peace").

עַל יִשְׂרָאֵל עַמְּךָ

"upon Israel your people"	יִשְׂרָאֵל means _____. עַמְּךָ means "your people" or "your nation." עַם means _____. ךָ is an ending that means _____. Look back at the שָׁלוֹם רָב prayer on page 78. Underline every word that means "people" or "nation." How many words did you underline? _____

וְטוֹב בְּעֵינֶיךָ לְבָרֵךְ אֶת עַמְּךָ יִשְׂרָאֵל

"and may it be good in your eyes to bless your people Israel"	וְטוֹב means "and may it be good." בְּעֵינֶיךָ means "in your eyes." בְּ is a prefix meaning _____. ךָ is a suffix meaning _____.

שִׂים שָׁלוֹם

The prayer for peace recited in the morning, שִׂים שָׁלוֹם ("grant peace"), seems to outline a formula for peace: a conscientious life, kindness, generosity, blessing, and compassion.

PRACTICE:

Read שִׂים שָׁלוֹם.

שִׂים שָׁלוֹם (בָּעוֹלָם),	Grant peace (in the world)
טוֹבָה וּבְרָכָה,	goodness and blessing,
חֵן וָחֶסֶד	graciousness and kindness
וְרַחֲמִים	and mercy (compassion)
עָלֵינוּ וְעַל כָּל יִשְׂרָאֵל עַמֶּךָ.	upon us and upon all Israel Your people.
בָּרְכֵנוּ, אָבִינוּ, כֻּלָּנוּ כְּאֶחָד,	Bless us, our Parent, all of us as one,
בְּאוֹר פָּנֶיךָ,	with the light of Your face,
כִּי בְאוֹר פָּנֶיךָ	for with the light of Your face,
נָתַתָּ לָּנוּ, יְיָ אֱלֹהֵינוּ,	You gave us, Adonai our God,
תּוֹרַת חַיִּים, וְאַהֲבַת חֶסֶד,	the Torah of life, and a love of kindness,
וּצְדָקָה וּבְרָכָה	and righteousness and blessing
וְרַחֲמִים,	and mercy (compassion),
וְחַיִּים וְשָׁלוֹם.	and life and peace.
וְטוֹב בְּעֵינֶיךָ	And may it be good in Your eyes
לְבָרֵךְ אֶת עַמְּךָ	to bless Your people
יִשְׂרָאֵל (וְאֶת כָּל הָעַמִּים)	Israel (and all peoples)
בְּכָל עֵת וּבְכָל שָׁעָה	at every time and at every hour
בִּשְׁלוֹמֶךָ.	with Your peace.
בָּרוּךְ אַתָּה יְיָ,	Blessed are You, Adonai,
הַמְבָרֵךְ אֶת עַמּוֹ	who blesses God's people
יִשְׂרָאֵל בַּשָּׁלוֹם.	Israel with peace.

Think About It!

Just as in שָׁלוֹם רָב we extend the wish for peace to all others, so here, too, can we add בָּעוֹלָם ("throughout the world") to include everyone in the blessing for peace.

BUILDING YOUR VOCABULARY

Read through the words in the Prayer Dictionary. Are any familiar to you?

Complete the following Prayer Dictionary activities.

1. The עֲמִידָה begins with a blessing called אָבוֹת.
   Put a check next to the word related to אָבוֹת.

2. Write the English meaning of each word.

טוֹבָה _____

וְאַהֲבַת חֶסֶד _____

חֵן _____

Asking Favors

שִׂים שָׁלוֹם asks God to bless us with six favors or gifts. Below are the English meanings of the six gifts we ask of God. Write each one in the blank space next to its matching Hebrew word.

blessing   kindness   peace   mercy   goodness   graciousness

1. שָׁלוֹם _____

2. טוֹבָה _____

3. בְּרָכָה _____

4. חֵן _____

5. חֶסֶד _____

6. רַחֲמִים _____

Which of these gifts do you consider to be most important? Why?

_____

_____

What other favors or gifts would you ask of God?

_____

PRAYER DICTIONARY

שִׂים
grant, put

טוֹבָה
goodness

חֵן
graciousness

אָבִינוּ
our parent

כֻּלָּנוּ כְּאֶחָד
all of us as one

נָתַתָּ
you gave

תּוֹרַת חַיִּים
Torah of life

וְאַהֲבַת חֶסֶד
and a love of kindness

שִׂים שָׁלוֹם

"grant peace"

שִׂים usually means "put," but in this prayer we translate it as "grant."

The root of שִׂים is שׂימ.

The root שׂימ tells us that "put" is part of a word's meaning.

Read the first sentence of שָׁלוֹם רָב — the evening prayer for peace — and circle the word with the root שׂימ.

שָׁלוֹם רָב עַל יִשְׂרָאֵל עַמְּךָ תָּשִׂים לְעוֹלָם,
כִּי אַתָּה הוּא מֶלֶךְ אָדוֹן, לְכָל הַשָּׁלוֹם.

בָּרְכֵנוּ, אָבִינוּ, כֻּלָּנוּ כְּאֶחָד

"bless us, our parent, all of us as one"

Write the root of בָּרְכֵנוּ. _____ _____ _____

Words built on this root have "_____" as part of their meaning.

אָבִינוּ literally means "our father."

אָב means "father."

נוּ is an ending meaning _____.

Because God is neither male nor female, we translate אָבִינוּ as "our parent."

כֻּלָּנוּ כְּאֶחָד means "all of us as one."

כֻּלָּנוּ has two parts: כָּל ("all") and the ending נוּ ("us").

כְּאֶחָד means "as one."

כְּ means "as."

אֶחָד means _____.

Circle אֶחָד in the prayer below.

שְׁמַע יִשְׂרָאֵל יְיָ אֱלֹהֵינוּ יְיָ אֶחָד.

An Ethical Echo

In בִּרְכַּת שָׁלוֹם we ask for peace, for Israel and all the world. But we know that world peace is something that will not happen solely by God's hand. Working toward peace can start within the realm of our own homes. שְׁלוֹם בַּיִת ("peace in the home") is a central value in Judaism. Our tradition offers us prayers on this theme. Some ask for continued "love, tenderness, peace, and friendship" between husband and wife. Some ask for "light, joy, blessing, and intimacy" for all the members of the household. But even as we ask God for these gifts, we know that the secret to possessing them resides in us.

What do you think שְׁלוֹם בַּיִת looks like and feels like?

_____

Do you think that שְׁלוֹם בַּיִת can lead to peace in the world? Why? How?

_____

תּוֹרַת חַיִּים, וְאַהֲבַת חֶסֶד

"the Torah of life, and a love of kindness"

תּוֹרָה is, of course, Torah.

חַיִּים, we have learned, means "life."

תּוֹרַת חַיִּים means "the Torah of life."

This phrasing is an example of s'michut, a Hebrew construct indicating the possessive form, in which two nouns combine to create a new term. The construct "The Torah of life" could be interpreted as "the law of life," "the Torah telling the story of life," or "the Torah makes life better." Which explanation do you like best? Why?

_____

וְאַהֲבַת חֶסֶד is another example of s'michut, as is שְׁלוֹם בַּיִת ("peace in the home").

Circle the three root letters in וְאַהֲבַת.

Words built on this root have "_____" as part of their meaning.

Earlier in the book you learned a prayer that tells us to love God.

Write its name in English letters. _____

A Personal Prayer

The עֲמִידָה is a compilation of communal prayers expressing the values and wishes of the Jewish people. Now, at the end of the עֲמִידָה, we are invited to add a personal, silent prayer, perhaps our own words or perhaps those from the prayer אֱלֹהַי נְצֹר. Written seventeen hundred years ago, this personal prayer serves as a model for what we add ourselves. In it, we ask for God's help in following the commandments and in choosing our words carefully.

PRACTICE:

Read the personal prayer at the end of the עֲמִידָה.

אֱלֹהַי, נְצֹר לְשׁוֹנִי מֵרָע,	My God, guard my tongue from evil,
וּשְׂפָתַי מִדַּבֵּר מִרְמָה,	and my lips from speaking deceitful things,
וְלִמְקַלְלַי נַפְשִׁי תִדּוֹם,	and let my soul be still to those who (may) curse m
וְנַפְשִׁי כֶּעָפָר לַכֹּל תִּהְיֶה.	may my soul be like dust to everyone.
פְּתַח לִבִּי בְּתוֹרָתֶךָ,	Open my heart to Your Torah,
וּבְמִצְוֹתֶיךָ תִּרְדּוֹף נַפְשִׁי.	and let my soul pursue Your mitzvot.
וְכָל הַחוֹשְׁבִים עָלַי רָעָה,	And may all who design bad things for me,
מְהֵרָה הָפֵר עֲצָתָם	have their counsel foiled,
וְקַלְקֵל מַחֲשַׁבְתָּם.	and their designs cursed.
עֲשֵׂה לְמַעַן שְׁמֶךָ,	Do (all this) because of Your name,
עֲשֵׂה לְמַעַן יְמִינֶךָ,	do (it) for the sake of Your right hand (strength),
עֲשֵׂה לְמַעַן קְדֻשָּׁתֶךָ.	and do (it) on account of Your holiness.
עֲשֵׂה לְמַעַן תּוֹרָתֶךָ.	Do (it) because of Your Torah.
לְמַעַן יֵחָלְצוּן יְדִידֶיךָ,	Thus those whom You love may be free;
הוֹשִׁיעָה יְמִינְךָ וַעֲנֵנִי.	may Your right hand save and answer me.
יִהְיוּ לְרָצוֹן אִמְרֵי פִי	May the words of my mouth and the private
וְהֶגְיוֹן לִבִּי לְפָנֶיךָ,	thought in my heart be acceptable to You,
יְיָ צוּרִי וְגוֹאֲלִי.	Adonai, my Rock and my Redeemer.

No matter what your prayer, end it, as Jews have done for thousands of years, with a prayer for peace:

עֹשֶׂה שָׁלוֹם בִּמְרוֹמָיו,	May God who makes peace in the heavens,
הוּא יַעֲשֶׂה שָׁלוֹם עָלֵינוּ,	make peace for us
וְעַל כָּל יִשְׂרָאֵל. וְאִמְרוּ אָמֵן.	and for all Israel. And say, Amen.

In a final flourish, and to show that we are symbolically taking our leave from a Sovereign, traditional observance calls for us to take three steps back, and bow to the left, the right, and the center. The עֲמִידָה is complete.

אֵין כָּמוֹךְ 15
אַב הָרַחֲמִים

אֵין כָּמוֹךְ

Each week, Jews all over the world gather to read the Torah — some on Mondays, Thursdays, and Shabbat mornings; some on Shabbat mornings only; others on Friday nights. This has been Jewish practice for almost two thousand five hundred years, since the Jewish people returned under the leadership of Ezra the priest to Jerusalem from exile in Babylonia. The same weekly פָּרָשָׁה ("portion") is read around the world, whether in Bangkok, Berlin, or Baltimore. Although it is embedded in today's synagogue service, public Torah reading predates communal prayer and is a founding ritual of the Jewish people.

The Torah service has evolved into a highly choreographed ceremony, from the way the Torah is taken out of the Ark, to the way it is dressed, held, carried around, and read. And no wonder why. The Torah is the touchstone, the banner, of the Jewish people. It is what has kept us whole throughout all of our wanderings.

We begin the Torah service with a paean to God, mostly verses from Psalms. Before the עֲמִידָה we ask, מִי כָמֹכָה — Who is like You, God? Here, we answer, אֵין כָּמוֹךְ — There is none like You.

PRACTICE:

Read אֵין כָּמוֹךְ.

אֵין כָּמוֹךְ	There is none like You, Adonai,
בָאֱלֹהִים, יְיָ,	among the gods (other people worship),
וְאֵין כְּמַעֲשֶׂיךָ.	and there are no deeds like Yours.
מַלְכוּתְךָ מַלְכוּת כָּל עֹלָמִים,	Your sovereignty is an eternal sovereignty,
וּמֶמְשַׁלְתְּךָ בְּכָל דּוֹר וָדֹר.	and Your reign is from generation to generation.
יְיָ מֶלֶךְ, יְיָ מָלָךְ,	Adonai is Sovereign (Ruler), Adonai ruled,
יְיָ יִמְלֹךְ לְעוֹלָם וָעֶד.	Adonai will rule forever and ever.
יְיָ עֹז לְעַמּוֹ יִתֵּן,	May Adonai give strength to our people,
יְיָ יְבָרֵךְ אֶת עַמּוֹ בַשָּׁלוֹם.	may Adonai bless our people with peace.

PRAYER DICTIONARY

אֵין
(there is/are) none

כָּמוֹךָ
like you

(כְּ) מַעֲשֶׂיךָ
(like) your deeds

מַלְכוּתְךָ
your sovereignty

וּמֶמְשַׁלְתְּךָ
and your reign

מֶלֶךְ
(is) sovereign (ruler)

מָלַךְ
ruled

יִמְלֹךְ
will rule

BUILDING YOUR VOCABULARY

You have learned that the suffix ךָ means "you" or "yours." In this prayer, as in many others, ךָ demonstrates God's possession.

Use the Prayer Dictionary to fill in the missing English words on the chart below. The first example has been completed for you.

like you	כָּמוֹךָ	ךָ	כְּמוֹ+
	מֶמְשַׁלְתְּךָ	ךָ	מֶמְשַׁלְתְּ+
	מַלְכוּתְךָ	ךָ	מַלְכוּת+
	מַעֲשֶׂיךָ	ךָ	מַעֲשֶׂי+

PAST, PRESENT, FUTURE

Each word next to יְיָ below is built on the root מלכ ("rule"). On each line, write whether it is past, present, or future tense.

tense

_____ יְיָ יִמְלֹךְ

_____ יְיָ מָלַךְ

_____ יְיָ מֶלֶךְ

Reread the אֵין כָּמוֹךָ prayer on page 86. Circle all the words built on the root מלכ.

How many words did you circle? _____

Prayer Building Blocks

אֵין כָּמוֹךָ בָאֱלֹהִים

"there is none like you among the gods [other people worship]"

אֵין means "(there is) none."

כָּמוֹךָ is made up of two parts:

כְּמוֹ means "like."

ךָ is a suffix meaning "you" or "your."

Sometimes, when you add a suffix to a word, it changes the word's letters or vowels (כְּמוֹ + ךָ = כָּמוֹךָ).

בָאֱלֹהִים means "among the gods."

בָ is a prefix meaning "among the" or "in the."

אֱלֹהִים means "gods."

The word "gods" is written with a lower case "g" because it refers to pagan gods that people worshipped in ancient times. We write the name of our God with a capital "G" because there is only One God.

The שְׁמַע expresses this belief: שְׁמַע יִשְׂרָאֵל: יְיָ אֱלֹהֵינוּ, יְיָ אֶחָד.

Write the English meaning of the שְׁמַע below.

_____

Think About It!

The Torah service begins with a reference to God, not the Torah itself. Why begin with God? Because tradition tells us that Torah is the word of God, the story of the Jewish people, and the divine will as told by God. Some say it is inspired by God, created and recorded by the Jewish people in response to their ongoing experiences of God. Others offer that it is the Jewish people's collective, dynamic imagination of God.

Here, too, as with so many other blessings, we end our praise of God with a call for peace.

וְאֵין כְּמַעֲשֶׂיךָ

"and there are no deeds like yours"

אֵין, we know, means "(there is/are) none."

The prefix וְ means _____.

כְּמַעֲשֶׂיךָ means "like your deeds."

We have just learned that the word כְּמוֹ means "like."

כְּ, the shorter form of the word כְּמוֹ, also means "like."

מַעֲשֶׂיךָ means "your deeds."

מַעֲשֶׂיךָ is built on the root עשׂה.

עשׂה tells us that "do" or "make" is part of a word's meaning.

Circle the root letters in each word below.

לְמַעֲשֶׂה   עֹשֶׂה   יַעֲשֶׂה   שֶׁעָשָׂה

Now circle the words built on the root עשׂה in the prayer below.

עֹשֶׂה שָׁלוֹם בִּמְרוֹמָיו, הוּא יַעֲשֶׂה שָׁלוֹם עָלֵינוּ,
וְעַל כָּל יִשְׂרָאֵל וְאִמְרוּ אָמֵן.

From the Sources

The prayer phrase יְיָ מֶלֶךְ, יְיָ מָלָךְ, יְיָ יִמְלֹךְ is a compilation of verses from different parts of the Bible.

Read each biblical verse below and circle the phrase that appears in אֵין כָּמוֹךָ.
(Remember: God's name can be written as יְיָ or יְהֹוָה.)

Psalms 10:16   יְהֹוָה מֶלֶךְ עוֹלָם וָעֶד אָבְדוּ גוֹים מֵאַרְצוֹ:

אָמְרוּ בַגּוֹים יְהֹוָה מָלָךְ אַף תִּכּוֹן
Psalms 96:10   תֵּבֵל בַּל תִּמּוֹט יָדִין עַמִּים בְּמֵישָׁרִים:

Exodus 15:18   יְהֹוָה יִמְלֹךְ לְעֹלָם וָעֶד:

There is no single verse in the Bible that says God is, was, and will always be Sovereign, yet the prayer expresses all these ideas in one sentence. Why do you think the prayer contains all these thoughts?

_____

_____

אַב הָרַחֲמִים

We begin the Torah service by speaking of God's uniqueness. We continue by invoking God, the merciful. At this moment, just before opening the doors of the Ark to take out the Torah, we add the prayer that was always in the hearts and minds of the Jews in exile: God, rebuild Jerusalem. Take us home.

PRACTICE:

Read אַב הָרַחֲמִים.

אַב הָרַחֲמִים,	Merciful Parent,
הֵיטִיבָה בִרְצוֹנְךָ אֶת צִיּוֹן;	favor Zion with Your goodness;
תִּבְנֶה חוֹמוֹת יְרוּשָׁלָיִם.	rebuild the walls of Jerusalem.
כִּי בְךָ לְבַד בָּטָחְנוּ,	For in You alone do we trust,
מֶלֶךְ אֵל רָם וְנִשָּׂא,	Sovereign God, high and exalted,
אֲדוֹן עוֹלָמִים.	eternal Ruler.

From the Sources

אַב הָרַחֲמִים asks God to favor Zion (Jerusalem) with goodness and to rebuild it. The words come from Psalm 51, written two thousand five hundred years ago, shortly after the destruction of the First Temple in 586 BCE.

הַתִּקְוָה

Moved by the swelling of Zionist passions all over Europe, and by the age-old dream of finally going home, a young Naftali Herz Imber wrote a poem that would become the unofficial anthem of the State of Israel eighty years later. His notes indicate he was visiting Jerusalem when he composed it.

Underline יְרוּשָׁלַיִם and צִיּוֹן wherever they appear in the poem.

PRACTICE:

Read הַתִּקְוָה.

כָּל עוֹד בַּלֵּבָב פְּנִימָה	In its inward heart
נֶפֶשׁ יְהוּדִי הוֹמִיָּה	The soul of the Jew trembles
וּלְפַאֲתֵי מִזְרָח קָדִימָה	To the far reaches of the East,
עַיִן לְצִיּוֹן צוֹפִיָּה.	Its eye looks toward Zion.
עוֹד לֹא אָבְדָה תִּקְוָתֵנוּ	Our hope is not lost
הַתִּקְוָה בַּת שְׁנוֹת אַלְפַּיִם	It is the hope of two thousand years:
לִהְיוֹת עַם חָפְשִׁי בְּאַרְצֵנוּ	That we would be a free people in our land
אֶרֶץ צִיּוֹן וִירוּשָׁלָיִם.	The land of Zion and Jerusalem.

PRAYER DICTIONARY

הָרַחֲמִים
merciful, the mercy

יְרוּשָׁלַיִם
Jerusalem

בָּטַחְנוּ
we trust(ed)

BUILDING YOUR VOCABULARY

Write the number of the missing word to complete each prayer phrase.

1. יְרוּשָׁלַיִם   2. בָּטַחְנוּ   3. הָרַחֲמִים

אַב ____
merciful parent

____ תִּבְנֶה חוֹמוֹת
rebuild the walls of Jerusalem

כִּי בְךָ לְבַד ____
for in you alone we trust(ed)

Merciful Parent

God has many names in Jewish tradition. In this prayer, said just before we open the Ark for the Torah service, we call to God as a merciful parent — אַב הָרַחֲמִים.

The root of הָרַחֲמִים is רחם.

The root רחם indicates that "mercy" or "compassion" is part of a word's meaning.

God is sometimes referred to by three other names, all expressing the idea of compassion. The names are:

God full of mercy   אֵל מָלֵא רַחֲמִים

the merciful One   הָרַחֲמָן

compassionate and gracious God   אֵל רַחוּם וְחַנּוּן

Circle the root letters רחם in each of God's names above.

Look through earlier chapters in this book and write at least two other names for God.

_____

16 כִּי מִצִּיּוֹן לְךָ יְיָ

The Ark is open and the congregation rises. The pageant is about to begin. As we prepare to take out the Torah and carry it around the synagogue in grand procession, this prayer reminds us of the days when the Ark of the Covenant (with the Ten Commandments inside) was carried through the desert after the Exodus from Egypt on the way to the Holy Land. Moses, accompanying it at the head of the legions of people, would proclaim: "Children of Israel, don't be afraid. Your enemies will flee from you." So, too, we are meant to feel invincible in the presence of the Torah.

Unlike today, in ancient times the Torah scroll was not kept in the synagogue proper but rather in an adjoining room. It was carried in for the Torah reading. This choreographed entrance dramatized the connection between the Ark housing the Torah and the Ark housing the Ten Commandments, and it united the generations of the Jewish people.

כִּי מִצִּיּוֹן

PRACTICE:

Read כִּי מִצִּיּוֹן.

כִּי מִצִּיּוֹן תֵּצֵא תוֹרָה,
וּדְבַר יְיָ מִירוּשָׁלָיִם.

For out of Zion shall go forth Torah,
and the word of God from Jerusalem.

בָּרוּךְ שֶׁנָּתַן תוֹרָה
לְעַמּוֹ יִשְׂרָאֵל בִּקְדֻשָּׁתוֹ.

Blessed is the One, who gave the Torah
to God's people Israel in holiness.

PRAYER DICTIONARY

מִצִּיּוֹן	from Zion
תּוֹרָה	Torah, teaching
וּדְבַר	and the word of
מִירוּשָׁלָיִם	from Jerusalem
שֶׁנָּתַן	who gave
לְעַמּוֹ	to God's people
בִּקְדֻשָּׁתוֹ	in God's holiness

BUILDING YOUR VOCABULARY

Study the Prayer Dictionary. Then cover it and draw a line from each Hebrew word to its English meaning.

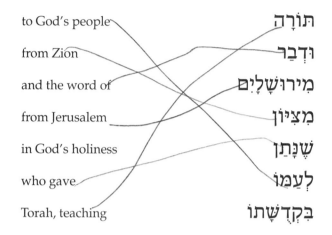

to God's people
from Zion
and the word of
from Jerusalem
in God's holiness
who gave
Torah, teaching

תּוֹרָה
וּדְבַר
מִירוּשָׁלָיִם
מִצִּיּוֹן
שֶׁנָּתַן
לְעַמּוֹ
בִּקְדֻשָּׁתוֹ

In the Synagogue

As the Ark is opened, some congregations add the following words from the Torah *(NUMBERS 10:35)* before כִּי מִצִּיּוֹן.

וַיְהִי בִּנְסֹעַ הָאָרֹן	When the Ark was carried forward,
וַיֹּאמֶר מֹשֶׁה:	Moses said:
קוּמָה יְיָ	Arise, Adonai;
וְיָפֻצוּ אֹיְבֶיךָ,	may Your enemies be scattered,
וְיָנֻסוּ מְשַׂנְאֶיךָ מִפָּנֶיךָ.	may Your foes be driven to flight.

Other congregations do not mention war or the Jews' enemies, but add:

הָבוּ גֹדֶל לֵאלֹהֵינוּ	Let us declare God's greatness
וּתְנוּ כָבוֹד לַתּוֹרָה.	and give honor to the Torah.

Which version of the prayer is found in *your* synagogue's prayer book?

WHAT'S MISSING?

Circle the word that completes each sentence.

לְעַמּוֹ	מִירוּשָׁלָיִם	מִצִּיּוֹן	1. כִּי _____ תֵּצֵא תוֹרָה *from Zion*
מִצִּיּוֹן	מִירוּשָׁלָיִם	תוֹרָה	2. וּדְבַר יְיָ _____ *from Jerusalem*
תוֹרָה	יִשְׂרָאֵל	יְיָ	3. בָּרוּךְ שֶׁנָּתַן _____ *Torah*
וּדְבַר	מִצִּיּוֹן	יִשְׂרָאֵל	4. לְעַמּוֹ _____ בִּקְדֻשָּׁתוֹ *Israel*

OUT OF ORDER

Number the seven words from the first line of כִּי מִצִּיּוֹן in the correct order.

מִצִּיּוֹן ◯ תוֹרָה ◯ וּדְבַר ◯ תֵּצֵא ◯

כִּי ◯ יְיָ ◯ מִירוּשָׁלָיִם ◯

Number the six words from the second line of כִּי מִצִּיּוֹן in the correct order.

יִשְׂרָאֵל ◯ לְעַמּוֹ ◯ שֶׁנָּתַן ◯ בָּרוּךְ ◯

בִּקְדֻשָּׁתוֹ ◯ תוֹרָה ◯

Think About It!

The Hebrew name for the bible — תַּנַ"ךְ — is an acronym. The Torah (ת-תוֹרָה) comprises the first part; the Prophets (נ-נְבִיאִים), for example, Isaiah and Jeremiah, comprises the second; and Writings (כ,ך-כְּתוּבִים), for example, the Psalms and Song of Songs, the third.

מִצִּיּוֹן

"from Zion"

What does the prefix מִ mean? _____

Zion is another name for Jerusalem.

What does מִירוּשָׁלַיִם mean? _____

וּדְבַר

"and the word of"

What does the prefix וּ mean? _____

דְּבַר means "the word of."

Read the following sentences and circle all the words built on the root דבר ("speak," "word," or "thing").

1. וְהָיוּ הַדְּבָרִים הָאֵלֶּה, אֲשֶׁר אָנֹכִי מְצַוְּךָ הַיּוֹם, עַל לְבָבֶךָ.
2. בָּרוּךְ אַתָּה יְיָ, הָאֵל הַנֶּאֱמָן בְּכָל דְּבָרָיו.
3. וְעֵינֵינוּ תִרְאֶינָה מַלְכוּתֶךָ כַּדָּבָר הָאָמוּר בְּשִׁירֵי עֻזֶּךָ.
4. וְדָבָר אֶחָד מִדְּבָרֶיךָ אָחוֹר לֹא יָשׁוּב רֵיקָם.
5. הָאֵל הַנֶּאֱמָן, הָאוֹמֵר וְעוֹשֶׂה, הַמְדַבֵּר וּמְקַיֵּם.

Think About It!

In Hebrew, we refer to the Ten Commandments as עֲשֶׂרֶת הַדִּבְּרוֹת.

Circle the root letters in the second word: הַדִּבְּרוֹת.

What does עֲשֶׂרֶת mean? _____

מִירוּשָׁלַיִם

"from Jerusalem"

While traditionally we believe that the Torah was given to the Jewish people in the wilderness on Mount Sinai, the prophet Isaiah imagines that the Torah will be given to *all* people at the end of time on the hills of Jerusalem —

כִּי מִצִּיּוֹן תֵּצֵא תוֹרָה, וּדְבַר יְיָ מִירוּשָׁלָיִם

At that time, the peoples of the world will "beat their swords into plowshares and their spears into pruning hooks" *(Isaiah 2:3–4)*.

Do you think sharing the Torah would lead to peace? Explain your answer.

_____

_____

Read the lines below and underline the Hebrew word for Jerusalem in each.

1. וּבְנֵה יְרוּשָׁלַיִם עִיר הַקֹּדֶשׁ בִּמְהֵרָה בְיָמֵינוּ.

2. אַב הָרַחֲמִים, הֵיטִיבָה בִרְצוֹנְךָ אֶת צִיּוֹן, תִּבְנֶה חוֹמוֹת יְרוּשָׁלָיִם.

3. תִּתְגַּדַּל וְתִתְקַדַּשׁ בְּתוֹךְ יְרוּשָׁלַיִם עִירְךָ.

4. בָּרוּךְ אַתָּה יְיָ, בּוֹנֵה בְרַחֲמָיו יְרוּשָׁלַיִם, אָמֵן.

5. שִׂמְחוּ אֶת יְרוּשָׁלַיִם וְגִילוּ בָהּ כָּל אֹהֲבֶיהָ.

The Western Wall and Dome of the Rock in Jerusalem

שֶׁנָּתַן

"who gave"	שֶׁנָּתַן is made up of two parts:
	שֶׁ is a prefix meaning "who" or "that."
	נָתַן means "gave."
	בָּרוּךְ שֶׁנָּתַן תּוֹרָה means "blessed is the One who gave the Torah."

לְעַמּוֹ

"to God's people"	לְ is a prefix meaning "to."
	עַמּוֹ means "God's people."
	עַם means "people" or "nation."
	וֹ at the end of a word means "his."
	As God is neither male nor female, we translate לְעַמּוֹ as "to God's people."

בִּקְדֻשָּׁתוֹ

"in God's holiness"	בְּ is a prefix meaning "in."
	קְדֻשָּׁה means "holiness."
	קְדֻשָּׁתוֹ means "God's holiness."
	בִּקְדֻשָּׁתוֹ means _____.
	What is the root of בִּקְדֻשָּׁתוֹ? ___ ___ ___
	Circle the root letters קדשׁ in each word below.
	קָדְשְׁךָ מַקְדִּישִׁים הַקָּדוֹשׁ וַיְקַדֵּשׁ
	וּקְדוֹשִׁים קָדוֹשׁ
	Words built on the root קדשׁ have "_____" as part of their meaning.

Holding the Torah

PRACTICE:

Read the prayers we say when the Torah is taken out of the Ark.

Often, it is the bar or bat mitzvah who holds the Torah scroll in front of the entire congregation after it is taken from the Ark. With the Torah as our witness, standing before the sacred community of Israel, we once again declare our allegiance to God, and our worthiness to be the stewards of the Torah's words.

שְׁמַע יִשְׂרָאֵל:	Hear O Israel:
יְיָ אֱלֹהֵינוּ, יְיָ אֶחָד.	Adonai is our God, Adonai is one.
אֶחָד אֱלֹהֵינוּ, גָּדוֹל אֲדוֹנֵנוּ,	Our God is one and is great;
קָדוֹשׁ שְׁמוֹ.	God's name is holy.
גַּדְּלוּ לַיְיָ אִתִּי,	Acclaim Adonai with me,
וּנְרוֹמְמָה שְׁמוֹ יַחְדָּו.	and together let us exalt God's name.

During the recitation of the שְׁמַע and אֶחָד, the leaders stand facing the congregation. It is the practice in many congregations that, when reciting גַּדְּלוּ, the leaders turn to face the Ark and bow, along with the entire congregation. The procession of the Torah through the sanctuary now begins. The Torah can be carried around the *bimah*, around the entire synagogue, or any section in between. Everyone turns to keep the Torah in sight. Congregants on the ends of the aisles, and those who move there, often reach out to touch the Torah with their *tallit* or prayer book and kiss the part that touches the Torah.

Often, it is the bar or bat mitzvah who holds the Torah after it is taken from the Ark.

לְךָ יְיָ

As the Torah is carried through the sanctuary, it is accompanied by a song of praise to God. Even though the Torah is holy, and must be treated with the utmost respect, we should not mistake it for the Ultimate in holiness. So while we honor the Torah, we worship only God.

PRACTICE:

Read לְךָ יְיָ.

לְךָ, יְיָ, הַגְּדֻלָּה וְהַגְּבוּרָה	Yours, God, is the greatness, the power,
וְהַתִּפְאֶרֶת וְהַנֵּצַח וְהַהוֹד,	the glory, the victory, and the majesty;
כִּי כֹל בַּשָּׁמַיִם וּבָאָרֶץ,	for all that is in heaven and earth
לְךָ יְיָ הַמַּמְלָכָה	is Yours. Yours is the sovereignty, God;
וְהַמִּתְנַשֵּׂא	You are supreme
לְכֹל לְרֹאשׁ.	over all.

In the Synagogue

The Torah is placed on the reading table, often on the *bimah*. A flurry of activity prepares it for reading. The rabbi, cantor, Torah reader, or a congregant help undress it. They take off the *yad*, the decorative pointer that helps the reader keep track in the text. They remove the Torah cover and untie its wimple, the cloth binder wound around the waist of the Torah to keep it from unraveling. Now they are ready. The Torah reading is about to begin.

Handsome garments and decorations both protect and beautify the Torah.

בִּרְכוֹת הַתּוֹרָה ⬠17

The Torah portion — *parashah* — is divided into sections, each one called an עֲלִיָה ("going up"), for the reading table is often designed to be higher than the seats. Often, there are two people who share the honor of an *aliyah*: the one who reads the Torah and the one who says the blessings before and after each section is read. The blessings begin the way the morning service began, with a call to praise God and the congregational response.

Blessing before the Torah Reading

PRACTICE:

Read the blessing before the Torah reading.

בָּרְכוּ אֶת יְיָ הַמְבֹרָךְ.

Bless Adonai, who is to be blessed.

בָּרוּךְ יְיָ

Blessed is Adonai,

הַמְבֹרָךְ לְעוֹלָם וָעֶד.

who is to be blessed forever and ever.

The blessing then thanks God for choosing us and giving us the gift of Torah.

בָּרוּךְ אַתָּה, יְיָ אֱלֹהֵינוּ,

Blessed are You, Adonai our God,

מֶלֶךְ הָעוֹלָם,

Sovereign of the world,

אֲשֶׁר בָּחַר בָּנוּ מִכָּל הָעַמִּים

for choosing us from all the nations

וְנָתַן לָנוּ אֶת תּוֹרָתוֹ.

and giving us God's Torah.

בָּרוּךְ אַתָּה יְיָ,

Blessed are You, Adonai,

נוֹתֵן הַתּוֹרָה.

who gives us the Torah.

Reconstructionists, who reconceive the concept of chosenness, say instead of the third and fourth lines:

אֲשֶׁר קֵרְבָנוּ לַעֲבוֹדָתוֹ

who has drawn us to Your service

וְנָתַן לָנוּ אֶת תּוֹרָתוֹ.

and has given us Your Torah.

PRAYER DICTIONARY

בָּחַר
chose (choosing)

בָּנוּ
us

מִכָּל
from all

הָעַמִּים
the nations

וְנָתַן
and gave (and giving)

לָנוּ
to us

תּוֹרָתוֹ
God's Torah

נוֹתֵן
gives

At the Root

נוֹתֵן and נָתַן share common root letters — נתנ ("give"). Circle the root letters in each word.

The word מַתָּנָה ("gift") is also built on the same root, although one of the root letters is missing.

Shavuot is known as the holiday of מַתַּן תּוֹרָה. Do you know why? *(Hint: Figure out what each word means.)*

_____

Aliyah

On Shabbat morning, there are traditionally seven *aliyot*, but the number can vary from congregation to congregation. An *aliyah* represents both a physical and a spiritual event. We use this same term when we are called up to the Torah or when we go to live in Israel. We don't just move to the Holy Land, we "make *aliyah*" — we go up to it.

Have you ever had an *aliyah* in the synagogue? If so, on what occasion?

_____

Do you remember your thoughts or feelings at the time? Write them here.

_____

_____

What connection do you see between being called to the Torah and moving to Israel?

_____

_____

Prayer Building Blocks

אֲשֶׁר בָּחַר בָּנוּ

"who
chose us"
("for
choosing us")

אֲשֶׁר means "who."

בָּחַר means "chose."

בָּנוּ means "us."

To whom do you think "us" refers?

_____

Some reject the notion of chosenness. Others say that God chose the Jews for special responsibilities. What do you think those responsibilities might be?

_____

_____

וְנָתַן לָנוּ אֶת תּוֹרָתוֹ

"and gave us
God's Torah"
("and giving us
God's Torah")

Write the English meaning of וְנָתַן. _____

תּוֹרָתוֹ is made up of two parts: תּוֹרָה and the word ending וֹ ("his").

Because God is neither male nor female, we translate תּוֹרָתוֹ as "God's Torah."

In the Synagogue

Traditionally, before reciting the blessing, the one honored with the *aliyah* holds a siddur or the end of a *tallit* and with it touches the words of the Torah indicated by the reader, kisses the siddur or *tallit*, takes hold of the עֲצֵי חַיִּים, the Torah's handles, and recites the blessing. This is done at both the beginning and the end of the *aliyah* although practice varies from congregation to congregation.

Special Blessings

מִי שֶׁבֵּרַךְ

Amid the *aliyot*, at this prime time in the Shabbat service, it is as if we feel just a little closer to God. A special prayer requesting renewed health and recovery for those who are ill is now recited. While traditionally it was recited for a single individual, increasingly it is said on behalf of all in need. Called the מִי שֶׁבֵּרַךְ (from its first words, "May the One who blessed"), the prayer gives those in the synagogue a moment to place the needs of their loved ones front and center before God and the community. And it assures those who are ill at home or in the hospital that they have not been forgotten.

PRACTICE:

Read the
מִי שֶׁבֵּרַךְ.

מִי שֶׁבֵּרַךְ אֲבוֹתֵינוּ	May the One who blessed our ancestors
אַבְרָהָם, יִצְחָק, וְיַעֲקֹב,	Abraham, Isaac, and Jacob,
שָׂרָה, רִבְקָה, רָחֵל, וְלֵאָה,	Sarah, Rebecca, Rachel, and Leah,
הוּא יְבָרֵךְ אֶת	bring blessings of health to
בֶּן\בַּת _____ וּ _____ .	son/daughter of _____ and _____.
הַקָּדוֹשׁ בָּרוּךְ הוּא	May the holy One
יִמָּלֵא רַחֲמִים עָלָיו\עָלֶיהָ.	be filled with compassion on his/her behalf
וְיִשְׁלַח לוֹ\לָהּ מְהֵרָה	and speedily send him/her
רְפוּאָה שְׁלֵמָה,	a complete recovery,
רְפוּאַת הַנֶּפֶשׁ,	a healing of spirit,
וּרְפוּאַת הַגּוּף,	and a healing of body,
בְּתוֹךְ שְׁאָר חוֹלֵי יִשְׂרָאֵל	in the midst of our people who are ill
וּבְתוֹךְ כָּל בְּנֵי אָדָם.	and all who are ill.
וְנֹאמַר אָמֵן.	And let us say Amen.

Have you ever stood in the synagogue and offered the name of someone who was ill? If so, do you remember how you felt?

Maftir and Maftirah

The last person called to the Torah is known as the מַפְטִיר (male reader) or the מַפְטִירָה (female reader). This is often the bar or bat mitzvah. Except for holidays and special *Shabbatot*, the מַפְטִיר or מַפְטִירָה recites the blessings for the Torah reading and repeats the last three verses of the last *aliyah*. This number can vary, especially for the bar or bat mitzvah, who may chant more of the Torah portion. The person honored with reading the הַפְטָרָה, the weekly portion of the Prophets that follows the Torah reading, is usually honored with מַפְטִיר.

Blessing after the Torah Reading

The blessing after the Torah reading — the blessing that concludes the *aliyah* — is poetic in its words praising God for the gift of Torah and the planting of eternal life within our midst. It conjures up images of Eden. We need not despair that we cannot return to Eden, this blessing seems to say. Eden, in the form of the Torah, has come to us. That may be one reason the handles of the Torah scroll are called עֲצֵי חַיִּים ("trees of life"), recalling the Tree of Life planted in the center of the Garden.

PRACTICE:

Read the blessing after the Torah reading.

בָּרוּךְ אַתָּה,	Blessed are You,
יְיָ אֱלֹהֵינוּ,	Adonai our God,
מֶלֶךְ הָעוֹלָם,	Sovereign of the universe,
אֲשֶׁר נָתַן לָנוּ	who gave us
תּוֹרַת אֱמֶת,	the Torah of truth,
וְחַיֵּי עוֹלָם נָטַע בְּתוֹכֵנוּ.	and implanted within us eternal life.
בָּרוּךְ אַתָּה יְיָ,	Blessed are You, Adonai,
נוֹתֵן הַתּוֹרָה.	who gives us the Torah.

An Ethical Echo

To be "kosher" for use in the synagogue, a Torah scroll must be perfect. No letter may be broken; none missing. The rabbis of old used to say that there are 600,000 letters in the Torah, just as there were 600,000 Jews at Sinai. And just as the Torah is incomplete if even one letter is missing, so the Jewish people cannot be whole if one Jew is left out, cut off, or missing. כָּל יִשְׂרָאֵל עֲרֵבִים זֶה בָּזֶה, our tradition tells us. All Jews are responsible one for the other. And so we are.

PRAYER DICTIONARY

תּוֹרַת
Torah of

אֱמֶת
truth

וְחַיֵּי
and life (of)

עוֹלָם
eternal, world

BUILDING YOUR VOCABULARY

Write the English meaning of each Hebrew phrase.

לְעוֹלָם וָעֶד _____

תּוֹרַת אֱמֶת _____

וְחַיֵּי עוֹלָם _____

מֶלֶךְ הָעוֹלָם _____

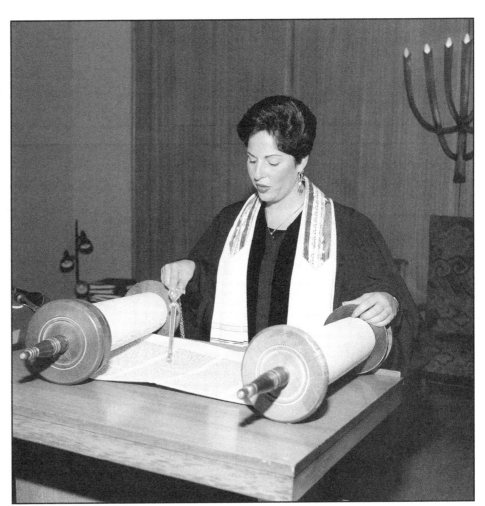

The Torah reader uses a *yad* or pointer to point to the words as she reads.

Prayer Building Blocks

אֲשֶׁר נָתַן לָנוּ תּוֹרַת אֱמֶת

"who gave us the Torah of truth"

נָתַן לָנוּ means _____ .

Words built on the root נתנ have "_____" as part of their meaning.

תּוֹרַת אֱמֶת means _____ .

In what way is the Torah a "Torah of truth"?

_____

וְחַיֵּי עוֹלָם

"and eternal life"

וְחַיֵּי means "and a life of."

עוֹלָם means both "eternal" and "world." Do you know the concluding hymn אֲדוֹן עוֹלָם? The name can be translated as "Eternal God" or "God of the World."

Read the following sentences and underline עוֹלָם in each one.

1. וְשִׁבְחֲךָ אֱלֹהֵינוּ מִפִּינוּ לֹא יָמוּשׁ לְעוֹלָם וָעֶד.

2. אֲדוֹן עוֹלָם אֲשֶׁר מָלַךְ בְּטֶרֶם כָּל יְצִיר נִבְרָא.

3. יִתְבָּרַךְ שִׁמְךָ בְּפִי כָּל חַי תָּמִיד לְעוֹלָם וָעֶד.

4. וַאֲנַחְנוּ נְבָרֵךְ יָה מֵעַתָּה וְעַד עוֹלָם.

וְזֹאת הַתּוֹרָה

More than anything else, the public reading of the scroll emphasizes that the Torah is the shared possession of the Jewish people. No one class, no one person, no one segment can lay claim to it. It belongs to everyone. So it was when it was given in the presence of all the people at Mount Sinai, and so it is today.

When we complete the reading, a congregant is called up to perform the honor of הַגְבָּהָה, lifting the Torah for all to see. The מַגְבִּיהַ (male) or מַגְבִּיהָה (female) lifts it high and shows its writing to the congregation, as if to say, "See, this is yours."

PRACTICE:

Read וְזֹאת הַתּוֹרָה.

וְזֹאת הַתּוֹרָה	And this is the Torah
אֲשֶׁר שָׂם מֹשֶׁה	that Moses placed
לִפְנֵי בְּנֵי יִשְׂרָאֵל,	before the people of Israel,
עַל פִּי יְיָ בְּיַד מֹשֶׁה.	by the word of Adonai through Moses.

These words come directly from the Torah itself, Deuteronomy 4:44–45. The Book of Deuteronomy is traditionally considered Moses' summation of the history of the Jewish people and of the *mitzvot* — the commandments. It is his swan song, his legacy before his death. We are told that "Moses summoned all the Israelites and said to them: Hear O Israel, the history, the laws, and the rules that I remind you of this day. Study them, and observe them faithfully" (*DEUTERONOMY 5:1*).

The scroll is then closed and wrapped by the person honored with גְּלִילָה, rolling up the Torah. The גּוֹלֵל (male) or גּוֹלֶלֶת (female) sets the Torah down on a specially designed stand while the person honored with מַפְטִיר reads the הַפְטָרָה from a printed book.

At the end of the Torah service, the scroll is lifted up high for the entire congregation to see. This ritual is called *hagbahah*.

18 בִּרְכוֹת הַהַפְטָרָה
אַשְׁרֵי
עֵץ חַיִּים הִיא

בִּרְכוֹת
הַהַפְטָרָה

After the Torah reading on Shabbat and holidays, we read a selection from the books of the Prophets — the הַפְטָרָה. Unlike the Torah, which is read from a scroll, the הַפְטָרָה is most often read from a printed book, thereby indicating a lesser level of sanctity. Even for the most traditional, only the Torah is thought to be the unmediated word of God. The Prophets speak God's word, but translated through their personal capacities and historical situations.

The meaning of the word הַפְטָרָה is not clear. It could indicate "completion," suggesting that the reading from the Prophets completes, and complements, the Torah reading. Usually, the הַפְטָרָה builds on the content of the *parashah* (even if the connection is as fine as a coincidence of words). Or it could mean "to expand upon," indicating an extension of the themes and message of the Torah reading.

The הַפְטָרָה is preceded by one blessing, and traditionally followed by four. The blessing before the prophetic reading speaks, appropriately, of how God chose the prophets and welcomed their prophecy.

PRACTICE:

Read the blessing
before the הַפְטָרָה.

בָּרוּךְ אַתָּה, יְיָ אֱלֹהֵינוּ,	Blessed are You, Adonai our God,
מֶלֶךְ הָעוֹלָם,	Sovereign of the universe,
אֲשֶׁר בָּחַר בִּנְבִיאִים טוֹבִים,	who chose good (faithful) prophets,
וְרָצָה בְדִבְרֵיהֶם	and was pleased with their words
הַנֶּאֱמָרִים בֶּאֱמֶת.	spoken in truth.
בָּרוּךְ אַתָּה יְיָ,	Blessed are You, Adonai,
הַבּוֹחֵר בַּתּוֹרָה,	the One who takes delight in (chooses) the Torah,

 continued

PRAYER DICTIONARY

בָּחַר
chose

(בְּ)נְבִיאִים
prophets

טוֹבִים
good (faithful)

הַנֶּאֱמָרִים
spoken

בֶּאֱמֶת
in truth

הַבּוֹחֵר
the one who chooses

עַבְדּוֹ
God's servant

עַמּוֹ
God's people

וְצֶדֶק
and righteousness (justice)

וּבְמשֶׁה עַבְדּוֹ, — and in Moses, God's servant,

וּבְיִשְׂרָאֵל עַמּוֹ, — and in Israel, God's people,

וּבִנְבִיאֵי הָאֱמֶת — and in prophets of truth

וָצֶדֶק. — and righteousness (justice).

BUILDING YOUR VOCABULARY

There are three sets of related words in the blessing before the הַפְטָרָה reading.

3	2	1
בֶּאֱמֶת	בִּנְבִיאִים	בָּחַר
הָאֱמֶת	וּבִנְבִיאֵי	הַבּוֹחֵר

Write the number of the related words next to their English meaning.

_____ prophets   _____ choose   _____ truth

Think About It!

The words צֶדֶק and צְדָקָה share the root צדק ("justice" or "righteousness").

Circle the root letters in each word below.

וָצֶדֶק   צֶדֶק   צְדָקָה

In Judaism, צְדָקָה is more than charity. It means doing what is just and right. The highest level of tzedakah, according to Maimonides' Ladder of Tzedakah, is when we give a needy person the tools to become self-sufficient.

How many times can you find the word צְדָקָה on this tzedakah box?

אֲשֶׁר בָּחַר בִּנְבִיאִים טוֹבִים

"who chose good (faithful) prophets"

בָּחַר means "chose."

נְבִיאִים is the plural of נָבִיא.

Circle the part of נְבִיאִים that shows it is plural: נְבִיאִים

נָבִיא means _____.

נְבִיאִים means _____.

טוֹבִים is an adjective describing נְבִיאִים.

Circle the part of טוֹבִים that shows it is plural: טוֹבִים

טוֹב means _____.

טוֹבִים means _____.

הַנֶּאֱמָרִים בֶּאֱמֶת

"spoken in truth"

הַנֶּאֱמָרִים means "spoken."

The root letters of הַנֶּאֱמָרִים are אמר.

אמר means "speak" or "say."

בֶּאֱמֶת means "in truth."

Read the following phrases aloud. Circle the words with the root אמר.

1. הָאֵל הַנֶּאֱמָן, הָאוֹמֵר וְעוֹשֶׂה

2. יִהְיוּ לְרָצוֹן אִמְרֵי פִי

3. חֲבֵרִים כָּל יִשְׂרָאֵל, וְנֹאמַר אָמֵן

4. אָז יֹאמְרוּ בַגּוֹיִם: "הִגְדִּיל יְיָ לַעֲשׂוֹת עִם אֵלֶּה"

5. בָּרוּךְ שֶׁאָמַר וְהָיָה הָעוֹלָם, בָּרוּךְ הוּא

הַבּוֹחֵר בַּתּוֹרָה

"the one who chooses the Torah"

הַבּוֹחֵר means "the one who chooses."

In this phrase, הַ is a prefix meaning "the one who."

בּוֹחֵר means _____.

הַבּוֹחֵר is built on the root בחר.

The root בחר tells us that "choose" is part of a word's meaning.

Below are lines from two prayers you have studied. Read each excerpt and circle all the words built on the root בחר. Then write the number of the line from each prayer next to the name of the prayer.

1. בָּרוּךְ אַתָּה, יְיָ אֱלֹהֵינוּ, מֶלֶךְ הָעוֹלָם, אֲשֶׁר בָּחַר בָּנוּ מִכָּל הָעַמִּים, וְנָתַן לָנוּ אֶת תּוֹרָתוֹ

2. כִּי בָנוּ בָחַרְתָּ וְאוֹתָנוּ קִדַּשְׁתָּ מִכָּל הָעַמִּים

_____ Kiddush

_____ Blessing before the Torah Reading

וּבְמֹשֶׁה עַבְדּוֹ

"and Moses, God's servant"

וּבְמֹשֶׁה means "and (in, with) Moses."

וּ is a prefix meaning _____.

מֹשֶׁה means _____.

עַבְדּוֹ means "God's servant."

עַבְדּוֹ is made up of two word-parts: עֶבֶד and the word ending וֹ ("his").
Because God is neither male nor female, we translate עַבְדּוֹ as "God's servant."
In what ways was Moses God's servant?

_____

_____

וּבְיִשְׂרָאֵל עַמּוֹ

"and Israel, God's people"

וּבְיִשְׂרָאֵל means "and (in, with) Israel."

וּ means _____.

יִשְׂרָאֵל means _____.

עַמּוֹ means "God's people."

וֹ at the end of a word means "his."

Because God is neither male nor female, we translate עַמּוֹ as "God's people."

Note: The Reconstructionist blessing before the haftarah does not mention God's choosing Israel but does recognize Moses' and the prophets' mission as a sacred one.

וּבִנְבִיאֵי הָאֱמֶת וָצֶדֶק

"and prophets of truth and righteousness (justice)"

וּבִנְבִיאֵי means "and prophets of."

וּ means _____.

נְבִיאֵי means "prophets of."

הָאֱמֶת means "the truth."

הָ means _____.

אֱמֶת means _____.

Read the following prayer excerpts. Circle the word אֱמֶת in each line.

1. וְטַהֵר לִבֵּנוּ לְעָבְדְּךָ בֶּאֱמֶת

2. אֲשֶׁר נָתַן לָנוּ תּוֹרַת אֱמֶת וְחַיֵּי עוֹלָם נָטַע בְּתוֹכֵנוּ

3. אֱמֶת מַלְכֵּנוּ, אֶפֶס זוּלָתוֹ

4. הוֹלֵךְ תָּמִים וּפֹעֵל צֶדֶק וְדֹבֵר אֱמֶת בִּלְבָבוֹ

וָצֶדֶק means "and righteousness" or "and justice."

וָ means _____.

צֶדֶק means _____.

Do you recognize line 2? Write the name of the prayer.

_____

Think About It!

We are not sure exactly when the הַפְטָרָה blessings were composed. The *Amora'im* — the rabbis whose commentaries on Jewish law are recorded in the Gemara — first referred to these blessings around the year 300 CE. So the הַפְטָרָה blessings are at least seventeen hundred years old.

Trope

The Torah scroll contains no vowels and no punctuation. To guide readers, scholars over the centuries codified vowels and punctuation known as *trope*. *Trope* parses words into phrases and sentences, lets the reader know where to pause and where to stop, and also serves as musical notations. *Trope* can be found in a *Ḥumash*, a printed version of the Torah, or a *tikun*, a book in which each Torah portion is laid out in two parallel columns. One column is in regular block Hebrew letters with vowels and *trope* signs, and the other column is as it would appear in a Torah scroll.

Although the same *trope* signs appear in Torah and haftarah text, they indicate different musical notes.

Some *trope* signs circled in blue

Blessings after the Haftarah Reading

The blessings after the הַפְטָרָה are more expansive than the single blessing before. The first of the four blessings speaks of God as faithful and reliable. Just as we are true to God, so God is true to us. It expresses the hope that God will remember the words we just read in the Prophets, which often speak of Israel's redemption.

The second blessing speaks of redemption itself, when the people Israel returns to its land; the third of the reestablishment of the throne of David and the coming of the messianic era; and the fourth of the sanctity of Shabbat.

In many congregations, it is common practice to recite only part of the first blessing and the complete fourth blessing.

Reconstructionists eliminate references to the restoration of King David's dynasty and to a personal Messiah and focus instead on the messianic era.

PRACTICE:

Read the four blessings after the הַפְטָרָה reading.

I

בָּרוּךְ אַתָּה, יְיָ אֱלֹהֵינוּ,	Blessed are You, Adonai our God,
מֶלֶךְ הָעוֹלָם,	Sovereign of the universe,
צוּר כָּל הָעוֹלָמִים,	rock of all eternity,
צַדִּיק בְּכָל הַדּוֹרוֹת,	righteous in all generations,
הָאֵל הַנֶּאֱמָן, הָאוֹמֵר וְעוֹשֶׂה,	the faithful God, the One who says and does,
הַמְדַבֵּר וּמְקַיֵּם,	the One who speaks and fulfills,
שֶׁכָּל דְּבָרָיו, אֱמֶת וָצֶדֶק.	for all God's words are truthful and just.
נֶאֱמָן אַתָּה הוּא, יְיָ אֱלֹהֵינוּ,	You are faithful, Adonai our God,
וְנֶאֱמָנִים דְּבָרֶיךָ,	and faithful are Your words,
וְדָבָר אֶחָד מִדְּבָרֶיךָ,	and not one of Your words
אָחוֹר לֹא יָשׁוּב רֵיקָם,	will return empty,
כִּי אֵל מֶלֶךְ נֶאֱמָן	for You are a faithful and compassionate
וְרַחֲמָן אָתָּה.	God and Sovereign.
בָּרוּךְ אַתָּה יְיָ,	Praised are You, Adonai,
הָאֵל הַנֶּאֱמָן בְּכָל דְּבָרָיו.	faithful in all Your words.

II

רַחֵם עַל צִיּוֹן	Have compassion for Zion,
כִּי הִיא בֵּית חַיֵּינוּ,	because it is the house of our lives.

 continued

וְלַעֲלוּבַת נֶפֶשׁ תּוֹשִׁיעַ

And to the poor in spirit

בִּמְהֵרָה בְיָמֵינוּ.

bring salvation swiftly.

בָּרוּךְ אַתָּה יְיָ,

Blessed are You, Adonai,

מְשַׂמֵּחַ צִיּוֹן בְּבָנֶיהָ.

who makes Zion rejoice in (because of) her children.

III

שַׂמְּחֵנוּ, יְיָ אֱלֹהֵינוּ,

Make us rejoice, Adonai our God,

בְּאֵלִיָּהוּ הַנָּבִיא עַבְדֶּךָ,

in Elijah the prophet Your servant,

וּבְמַלְכוּת בֵּית דָּוִד

and in the sovereignty of the House of David,

מְשִׁיחֶךָ,

Your anointed one.

בִּמְהֵרָה יָבֹא

May the Messiah come swiftly

וְיָגֵל לִבֵּנוּ.

so that our hearts may rejoice.

עַל כִּסְאוֹ לֹא יֵשֵׁב זָר

Let no improper person sit on that throne

וְלֹא יִנְחֲלוּ עוֹד אֲחֵרִים

and no improper person

אֶת כְּבוֹדוֹ,

inherit the majestic glory,

כִּי בְשֵׁם קָדְשְׁךָ נִשְׁבַּעְתָּ לּוֹ,

for You have promised, by Your holy Name,

שֶׁלֹּא יִכְבֶּה נֵרוֹ לְעוֹלָם וָעֶד.

that the light of David will never go out.

בָּרוּךְ אַתָּה יְיָ, מָגֵן דָּוִד.

Blessed are You, Adonai, the Shield of David.

IV

עַל הַתּוֹרָה, וְעַל הָעֲבוֹדָה,

For the Torah, and for the worship,

וְעַל הַנְּבִיאִים,

and for the prophets,

וְעַל יוֹם הַשַּׁבָּת הַזֶּה,

and for this Shabbat

שֶׁנָּתַתָּ לָּנוּ, יְיָ אֱלֹהֵינוּ,

that You have given us, Adonai our God,

לִקְדֻשָּׁה וְלִמְנוּחָה,

for holiness and for rest,

לְכָבוֹד וּלְתִפְאָרֶת,

for honor and glory,

עַל הַכֹּל, יְיָ אֱלֹהֵינוּ,

for all this, Adonai our God,

אֲנַחְנוּ מוֹדִים לָךְ,

we thank You

וּמְבָרְכִים אוֹתָךְ,

and bless You.

יִתְבָּרַךְ שִׁמְךָ בְּפִי

May Your name be blessed in the mouths

כָּל חַי תָּמִיד לְעוֹלָם וָעֶד.

of all the living, forever and ever.

בָּרוּךְ אַתָּה יְיָ,

Blessed are You, Adonai,

מְקַדֵּשׁ הַשַּׁבָּת.

who sanctifies the Sabbath.

אַשְׁרֵי

This lyrical psalm is a part of the early morning prayers, the prayers following the Torah reading, and the opening to the afternoon prayers. It is a hymn to God, a celebration of the psalmist's love for God, captured in acrostic form. In an acrostic, the initial letters of each line spell out a new word — often the author's name — or they form a pattern, in this case the Hebrew alphabet. (One interesting note: The letter *nun* is missing from this run of letters, and no one is quite sure why.)

PRACTICE:

Read the אַשְׁרֵי.

אַשְׁרֵי יוֹשְׁבֵי בֵיתֶךָ,
Happy are those who dwell in Your house;

עוֹד יְהַלְלוּךָ סֶּלָה.
they will praise You forever.

אַשְׁרֵי הָעָם שֶׁכָּכָה לּוֹ,
Happy are the people who are so favored;

אַשְׁרֵי הָעָם שֶׁיְיָ אֱלֹהָיו.
happy are the people whose God is Adonai.

תְּהִלָּה לְדָוִד.

אֲרוֹמִמְךָ אֱלוֹהַי הַמֶּלֶךְ, וַאֲבָרְכָה שִׁמְךָ לְעוֹלָם וָעֶד.

בְּכָל יוֹם אֲבָרְכֶךָּ, וַאֲהַלְלָה שִׁמְךָ לְעוֹלָם וָעֶד.

גָּדוֹל יְיָ וּמְהֻלָּל מְאֹד, וְלִגְדֻלָּתוֹ אֵין חֵקֶר.

דּוֹר לְדוֹר יְשַׁבַּח מַעֲשֶׂיךָ, וּגְבוּרֹתֶיךָ יַגִּידוּ.

הֲדַר כְּבוֹד הוֹדֶךָ, וְדִבְרֵי נִפְלְאֹתֶיךָ אָשִׂיחָה.

וֶעֱזוּז נוֹרְאֹתֶיךָ יֹאמֵרוּ וּגְדוּלָּתְךָ אֲסַפְּרֶנָּה.

זֵכֶר רַב טוּבְךָ יַבִּיעוּ, וְצִדְקָתְךָ יְרַנֵּנוּ.

חַנּוּן וְרַחוּם יְיָ, אֶרֶךְ אַפַּיִם וּגְדָל חָסֶד.

טוֹב יְיָ לַכֹּל, וְרַחֲמָיו עַל כָּל מַעֲשָׂיו.

יוֹדוּךָ יְיָ כָּל מַעֲשֶׂיךָ, וַחֲסִידֶיךָ יְבָרְכוּכָה.

כְּבוֹד מַלְכוּתְךָ יֹאמֵרוּ, וּגְבוּרָתְךָ יְדַבֵּרוּ.

לְהוֹדִיעַ לִבְנֵי הָאָדָם גְּבוּרֹתָיו, וּכְבוֹד הֲדַר מַלְכוּתוֹ.

מַלְכוּתְךָ מַלְכוּת כָּל עֹלָמִים, וּמֶמְשַׁלְתְּךָ בְּכָל דּוֹר וָדֹר.

סוֹמֵךְ יְיָ לְכָל הַנֹּפְלִים, וְזוֹקֵף לְכָל הַכְּפוּפִים.

עֵינֵי כֹל אֵלֶיךָ יְשַׂבֵּרוּ, וְאַתָּה נוֹתֵן לָהֶם אֶת אָכְלָם בְּעִתּוֹ.

פּוֹתֵחַ אֶת יָדֶךָ, וּמַשְׂבִּיעַ לְכָל חַי רָצוֹן.

צַדִּיק יְיָ בְּכָל דְּרָכָיו, וְחָסִיד בְּכָל מַעֲשָׂיו.

continued

117

קָרוֹב יְיָ לְכָל קֹרְאָיו, לְכָל אֲשֶׁר יִקְרָאֻהוּ בֶאֱמֶת.

רְצוֹן יְרֵאָיו יַעֲשֶׂה, וְאֶת שַׁוְעָתָם יִשְׁמַע וְיוֹשִׁיעֵם.

שׁוֹמֵר יְיָ אֶת כָּל אֹהֲבָיו, וְאֵת כָּל הָרְשָׁעִים יַשְׁמִיד.

תְּהִלַּת יְיָ יְדַבֶּר פִּי, וִיבָרֵךְ כָּל בָּשָׂר שֵׁם קָדְשׁוֹ, לְעוֹלָם וָעֶד.

וַאֲנַחְנוּ נְבָרֵךְ יָהּ,   And we will praise God,

מֵעַתָּה וְעַד עוֹלָם, הַלְלוּיָהּ.   now and forever. Hallelujah!

Think About It!

In the אַשְׁרֵי, "God's house" probably originally meant the Temple in Jerusalem. Today we can think of other explanations for "God's house." Give your own explanation.

_____

_____

_____

Can you imagine how even the oddest looking house can be God's house?

עֵץ
חַיִּים
הִיא

With poetic flourish and tunes that sound a note of sadness, we now return the Torah to the Ark. The wooden rollers that hold the Torah scroll are called עֲצֵי חַיִּים ("trees of life"). In prayer, the Torah itself is referred to as the Tree of Life. The reference recalls the plant in the Garden of Eden that is beyond our reach. God may have denied us reentry into the Garden of Eden, our liturgy tells us, but provided us with another, ever-accessible source of life, the Torah. As the Torah is returned to the Ark, we sing עֵץ חַיִּים הִיא, whose words are taken from the תַּנַ״ךְ (PROVERBS 3).

RACTICE:

Read
עֵץ חַיִּים הִיא.

עֵץ חַיִּים הִיא	It (the Torah) is a tree of life
לַמַּחֲזִיקִים בָּהּ,	to those who uphold it,
וְתֹמְכֶיהָ מְאֻשָּׁר.	and those who support it are happy.
דְּרָכֶיהָ דַרְכֵי נֹעַם,	Its ways are ways of pleasantness
וְכָל נְתִיבוֹתֶיהָ	and all its paths
שָׁלוֹם.	are peace.

Why do you think the prayer likens the Torah to a "tree of life"?

_____

_____

_____

BUILDING YOUR VOCABULARY

Study the Prayer Dictionary. Cover it, then write the English meaning of each Hebrew word below.

עֵץ _____

מְאֻשָּׁר _____

דְּרָכֶיהָ _____

דַרְכֵי _____

נֹעַם _____

PRAYER DICTIONARY

עֵץ
tree

חַיִּים
(of) life

מְאֻשָּׁר
happy

דְּרָכֶיהָ
its ways

דַרְכֵי
ways of

נֹעַם
pleasantness

שָׁלוֹם
peace

עֵץ חַיִּים הִיא לַמַּחֲזִיקִים בָּה

"it is a tree of life to those who uphold it"

עֵץ means _____.

חַיִּים means _____.

Fill in the missing words in English.

The Torah is a _____ to those who uphold it.

מֵאֻשָּׁר

"happy"

אֹשֶׁר means "happiness."

Read the following lines and circle the words meaning "happy."

אַשְׁרֵי יוֹשְׁבֵי בֵיתֶךָ עוֹד יְהַלְלוּךָ סֶּלָה.

אַשְׁרֵי הָעָם שֶׁכָּכָה לוֹ אַשְׁרֵי הָעָם שֶׁיְיָ אֱלֹהָיו.

How many words did you circle? _____

דְּרָכֶיהָ דַרְכֵי נֹעַם

"its ways are ways of pleasantness"

דְּרָכֶיהָ means "its ways."

דַרְכֵי means "ways of."

Both words are variations of דֶּרֶךְ ("road" or "way"). Circle the three letters meaning "road" or "way" in the words below:

דְּרָכֶיהָ   דַרְכֵי

Read the lines below and circle the words meaning "road" or "way."

1. צַדִּיק יְיָ בְּכָל דְּרָכָיו, וְחָסִיד בְּכָל מַעֲשָׂיו

2. בְּשִׁבְתְּךָ בְּבֵיתֶךָ וּבְלֶכְתְּךָ בַדֶּרֶךְ וּבְשָׁכְבְּךָ וּבְקוּמֶךָ

עָלֵינוּ 19

After the praises and petitions that punctuate the liturgy, עָלֵינוּ — the upbeat prayer found at the end of every service — describes a world free of strife and full of faith, a wonderland of goodness and godliness.

It signals the time to wind things up, to prepare to leave the place of prayer and reenter the world around us. Its opening notes evoke a sense of achievement (we did what we came to do), satisfaction (we did it well), and closure (almost time to go).

עָלֵינוּ recaps the complex of themes found throughout the service: pride and humility, imperfection and redemption, the unity of humanity and the distinctiveness of the Jewish people, God's immanence and God's transcendence. עָלֵינוּ sends us on our way believing that great, good things can happen in this world, and it is up to us to make it so.

PRACTICE:

Read עָלֵינוּ.

עָלֵינוּ לְשַׁבֵּחַ לַאֲדוֹן הַכֹּל,	It is our duty to praise the God of all,
לָתֵת גְּדֻלָּה	and to ascribe greatness
לְיוֹצֵר בְּרֵאשִׁית,	to the Maker of Creation,
שֶׁלֹּא עָשָׂנוּ	who has made us to be different from
כְּגוֹיֵי הָאֲרָצוֹת	the peoples of other lands,
וְלֹא שָׂמָנוּ	and made us to be different
כְּמִשְׁפְּחוֹת הָאֲדָמָה,	from the families of the earth.
שֶׁלֹּא שָׂם חֶלְקֵנוּ כָּהֶם,	God has made our destiny
וְגוֹרָלֵנוּ כְּכָל הֲמוֹנָם.	and our fortunes different.
וַאֲנַחְנוּ כּוֹרְעִים	And we bend our knees
וּמִשְׁתַּחֲוִים וּמוֹדִים	and we bow and give thanks
לִפְנֵי מֶלֶךְ מַלְכֵי הַמְּלָכִים,	before the Sovereign of all sovereigns,
הַקָּדוֹשׁ בָּרוּךְ הוּא.	the Holy One who is blessed.

 continued

שֶׁהוּא נוֹטֶה שָׁמַיִם	For God is the one who laid out the heavens
וְיוֹסֵד אָרֶץ,	and established the earth,
וּמוֹשַׁב יְקָרוֹ	with the dwelling place of divine glory
בַּשָּׁמַיִם מִמַּעַל,	in the heavens above,
וּשְׁכִינַת עֻזּוֹ	and the mighty Divine present
בְּגָבְהֵי מְרוֹמִים.	in the highest places.
הוּא אֱלֹהֵינוּ,	This is our God,
אֵין עוֹד.	there is no other.
אֱמֶת מַלְכֵּנוּ,	Truthfully our Sovereign,
אֶפֶס זוּלָתוֹ,	unique completely,
כַּכָּתוּב בְּתוֹרָתוֹ:	as it is written in the Torah:
וְיָדַעְתָּ הַיּוֹם	Know this day
וַהֲשֵׁבֹתָ אֶל לְבָבֶךְ,	and take it to your heart,
כִּי יְיָ הוּא הָאֱלֹהִים	that Adonai is God
בַּשָּׁמַיִם מִמַּעַל	in the heavens above
וְעַל הָאָרֶץ מִתָּחַת,	and on the earth,
אֵין עוֹד.	and there is no other.
וְנֶאֱמַר: וְהָיָה יְיָ	And it is said: Adonai
לְמֶלֶךְ עַל כָּל הָאָרֶץ,	is Sovereign over the entire earth;
בַּיּוֹם הַהוּא	on that day
יִהְיֶה יְיָ אֶחָד	Adonai will be One
וּשְׁמוֹ אֶחָד.	and the name of God shall be One.

In the Synagogue

One of our most ancient prayers (whose authorship is lost to antiquity), עָלֵינוּ was originally recited as part of the עֲמִידָה on Rosh Hashanah. It was during the Middle Ages, a time of persecution, banishment, and wandering, that this once-a-year prayer was elevated to a daily place of honor. What better way to respond to a world that was set against you than to conjure up a time when all people acknowledge and celebrate your God?

BUILDING YOUR VOCABULARY

Study the Prayer Dictionary. Cover it, then fill in the English meanings for the two names for God below.

אָדוֹן

_____

מֶלֶךְ מַלְכֵי הַמְּלָכִים

_____

Circle the three root letters in each word in the phrase מֶלֶךְ מַלְכֵי הַמְּלָכִים.

Many of the words in עָלֵינוּ end with the suffix נוּ ("us" or "our"). Circle all the words in the prayer ending with נוּ.

How many words did you circle? _____

Praying together as a community can give us a feeling of belonging and a sense that we are not alone in our prayers.

Prayer Variations

שֶׁנָּתַן לָנוּ   who gave us

תּוֹרַת אֱמֶת,   the Torah of truth,

וְחַיֵּי עוֹלָם   and eternal life

נָטַע בְּתוֹכֵנוּ   implanted within us

Reconstructionists use these words to replace the traditional words of עָלֵינוּ that thank God for "making us different from the peoples of other lands and different from the families of the earth."

Do you recognize the words the Reconstructionists use?

PRAYER DICTIONARY

עָלֵינוּ
it is our duty

לְשַׁבֵּחַ
to praise

(לְ)אָדוֹן
God, Ruler

הַכֹּל
of all

וַאֲנַחְנוּ
and we

וּמוֹדִים
and thank

מֶלֶךְ מַלְכֵי הַמְּלָכִים
Sovereign of sovereigns

הָאָרֶץ
the land

בַּיּוֹם הַהוּא
on that day

יִהְיֶה
will be

Praying Together

The word עָלֵינוּ can be translated in many ways: "It is our duty" or "We are called" or "It is up to us." They are all correct translations, each one pointing to a different way in which people view their relationship with God.

To say **"It is our duty"** to praise God means that we are in God's debt and in God's service. We owe God our praise. As creatures of our Creator, we are subjects to our Sovereign, who does beneficent things for us. God is therefore deserving of our praise and we are duty-bound to give it. Our praise is not quite commanded, but not quite freely given either.

To say **"We are called"** to praise God evokes a more voluntaristic response. Our awareness of God's goodness and God's greatness moves us. We are urged by our emotions and by the call of our people to respond to God's glory. We stand both in awe and in gratitude, and in response we freely offer our praise.

To say **"It is up to us"** highlights the unique role we can play in this world as God's emissaries. If not for us, this meaning seems to hint, whom can God rely on to speak such praise? If not for us, who will speak of the majestic work of Creation, of God's abundant goodness? If not for us, who will call upon humanity to preserve the ultimate hope that one day we will be united in a world of dignity, devotion, and peace?

These three readings take us from servant to witness to partner, a progression that richly reflects some of the many ways we are with God.

Religious school students learn how to pray as a community.

Prayer Building Blocks

וַאֲנַחְנוּ כּוֹרְעִים וּמִשְׁתַּחֲוִים וּמוֹדִים

"and we bend the knee and bow and thank God"

Circle the prefix that means "and" in the following words:

וַאֲנַחְנוּ   וּמִשְׁתַּחֲוִים   וּמוֹדִים

Do you remember the name of the blessing of thanksgiving in the עֲמִידָה? Write its name in English letters. _____

In the Synagogue

The most effective moments of prayer often involve the body as well as the spirit, for the movement of the body can enliven the spirit. In עָלֵינוּ, we don't just proclaim our faithfulness, we show it. We bend our knees when we say כּוֹרְעִים, bow from the waist when we say וּמִשְׁתַּחֲוִים, hold the bow or bow further when we say וּמוֹדִים, and stand upright again when we say לִפְנֵי מֶלֶךְ.

לִפְנֵי מֶלֶךְ מַלְכֵי הַמְּלָכִים

"before the Sovereign of sovereigns"

Why this honorific? In ancient times, rulers were called "king of kings." To drive home God's unique and superior status, the author chose this grand superlative, setting God above and beyond the highest of earthly rulers.

בַּיּוֹם הַהוּא יִהְיֶה יְיָ אֶחָד וּשְׁמוֹ אֶחָד

"on that day, Adonai will be one and God's name will be one"

בַּיּוֹם הַהוּא means "on that day."

יוֹם means "day."

In Hebrew, the names of the days of the week are constructed by adding sequential numbers (first, second, third) to the word יוֹם. Read the names of the days of the week in Hebrew.

יוֹם רְבִיעִי	יוֹם שְׁלִישִׁי	יוֹם שֵׁנִי	יוֹם רִאשׁוֹן
Wednesday	Tuesday	Monday	Sunday

יוֹם שַׁבָּת	יוֹם שִׁשִּׁי	יוֹם חֲמִישִׁי
Shabbat	Friday	Thursday

Back to the Sources

Some congregations add the following line from Pirkei Avot to the service:

עַל שְׁלשָׁה דְבָרִים — On three things

הָעוֹלָם עוֹמֵד: — our world stands:

עַל הַתּוֹרָה, — on Torah,

וְעַל הָעֲבוֹדָה, — on worship,

וְעַל גְּמִילוּת חֲסָדִים. — and on acts of loving-kindness. (PIRKEI AVOT 1:2)

Another quote from Pirkei Avot presents a different perspective. Read the selection:

עַל שְׁלשָׁה דְבָרִים — On three things

הָעוֹלָם עוֹמֵד: — our world stands:

עַל הַדִּין, — on justice,

וְעַל הָאֱמֶת, — on truth,

וְעַל הַשָּׁלוֹם. — and on peace. (PIRKEI AVOT 1:18)

Each quote presents a vision of how we can work to perfect the world and make it a better place. Which teaching would you rather follow? Why?

_____

_____

_____

20 קַדִּישׁ

The קַדִּישׁ is one of the most recognized prayers in all of Jewish liturgy. It is a graceful prayer that speaks of God's grandness. In an unhurried fashion, it heaps synonym upon synonym, calling for God's name to be celebrated around the world. Its rhythmic pace lulls the speaker; its responsive form calls to everyone in the room.

Surprisingly, although the קַדִּישׁ does not directly speak of death, it became a prayer for mourners. At our saddest moments, we speak words of promise and hope. The power of the prayer transcends its literal meaning and can be found instead in its resonance and history.

PRACTICE:

Read the Mourner's קַדִּישׁ.

יִתְגַּדַּל וְיִתְקַדַּשׁ	May God's name be great
שְׁמֵהּ רַבָּא	and may it be made holy
בְּעָלְמָא	in the world
דִּי בְרָא כִרְעוּתֵהּ,	created according to God's will.
וְיַמְלִיךְ מַלְכוּתֵהּ	May God rule
בְּחַיֵּיכוֹן וּבְיוֹמֵיכוֹן	in our own lives and our own days,
וּבְחַיֵּי דְכָל בֵּית יִשְׂרָאֵל,	and in the life of all the house of Israel,
בַּעֲגָלָא וּבִזְמַן קָרִיב,	swiftly and soon,
וְאִמְרוּ אָמֵן.	and say, Amen.
יְהֵא שְׁמֵהּ רַבָּא מְבָרַךְ	May God's great name be blessed
לְעָלַם וּלְעָלְמֵי עָלְמַיָּא.	forever and ever.
יִתְבָּרַךְ וְיִשְׁתַּבַּח	Blessed, praised,
וְיִתְפָּאַר וְיִתְרוֹמַם וְיִתְנַשֵּׂא	glorified, exalted, extolled,
וְיִתְהַדָּר וְיִתְעַלֶּה	honored, magnified,
וְיִתְהַלָּל שְׁמֵהּ דְּקֻדְשָׁא,	and adored be the name of the Holy One,
בְּרִיךְ הוּא.	blessed is God,

continued

לְעֵלָא מִן	though God is beyond
כָּל בִּרְכָתָא וְשִׁירָתָא,	all the blessings, songs,
תֻּשְׁבְּחָתָא וְנֶחֱמָתָא	adorations, and consolations
דַּאֲמִירָן בְּעָלְמָא,	that are spoken in the world,
וְאִמְרוּ אָמֵן.	and say, Amen.
יְהֵא שְׁלָמָא רַבָּא	May there be great peace
מִן שְׁמַיָּא	from heaven
וְחַיִּים עָלֵינוּ וְעַל כָּל יִשְׂרָאֵל,	and life for us and for all Israel,
וְאִמְרוּ אָמֵן.	and say, Amen.
עֹשֶׂה שָׁלוֹם בִּמְרוֹמָיו	May God who makes peace in the heavens,
הוּא יַעֲשֶׂה שָׁלוֹם	make peace
עָלֵינוּ וְעַל כָּל יִשְׂרָאֵל,	for us and for all Israel.
וְאִמְרוּ אָמֵן.	And say, Amen.

Judaism teaches us the importance of comforting those who have suffered a loss, for them and for us.

THE HEBREW-ARAMAIC CONNECTION

The words in the קַדִּישׁ may look difficult but, in fact, you already know many of them!

In the right-hand column below are Hebrew prayer words you have already learned. In the left-hand column are related Aramaic words from the קַדִּישׁ.

Write the number of the Hebrew word next to its related Aramaic word. *(Hint: Look for related roots.)*

ARAMAIC		HEBREW
בְּרִיךְ	_____	1. גְּדֻלָּה
בְּעָלְמָא	_____	2. קִדְּשָׁנוּ
וּבְחַיֵּי	_____	3. הָעוֹלָם
יִתְגַּדַּל	_____	4. מֶלֶךְ
קַדִּישׁ, וְיִתְקַדַּשׁ	_____	5. חַיִּים
וְיַמְלִיךְ	_____	6. בָּרוּךְ
שְׁלָמָא	_____	7. שָׁלוֹם

Think About It!

The קַדִּישׁ is written in Aramaic, the vernacular of the Jewish people during the earliest centuries of the common era. This choice of language enabled all who prayed to understand what they were saying. As time passed, and new native languages — such as Ladino, Yiddish, and English — developed among the Jews, the comforting familiarity of the words of the קַדִּישׁ helped preserve this Aramaic version. Today, many prayer books print the קַדִּישׁ in transliteration, so even those who cannot read Hebrew, and do not understand the words, can say this age-old prayer.

PRAYER DICTIONARY

קַדִּישׁ
holy

יִתְגַּדַּל
will be great

וְיִתְקַדַּשׁ
and will be holy

שְׁמֵהּ
God's name

בְּעָלְמָא
in the world

וְיַמְלִיךְ
and will rule

מַלְכוּתֵהּ
God's kingdom

PRAYER DICTIONARY

וּבְחַיֵּי	and in the life of
לְעָלַם	forever
וְיִשְׁתַּבַּח	and will be praised
בְּרִיךְ	blessed
בְּרְכָתָא	blessing
שְׁלָמָא	peace

AT THE ROOT

Next to each word from the קַדִּישׁ write the number of the root on which that word is built.

(Hint: You may have to use the same number twice.)

1. מלכ   2. קדשׁ   3. ברכ   4. שׁלמ   5. גדל

_____ בְּרִיךְ

_____ מַלְכוּתֵהּ

_____ יִתְגַּדַּל

_____ וְיִתְקַדַּשׁ

_____ בְּרְכָתָא

_____ וְיַמְלִיךְ

_____ קַדִּישׁ

_____ שְׁלָמָא

For each root, give its general meaning.

The first example has been completed for you.

1. מלכ   _____rule_____

2. קדשׁ   _____

3. ברכ   _____

4. שׁלמ   _____

5. גדל   _____

In the Synagogue

There are different versions of the קַדִישׁ, united by a common core. The prayer appears throughout the prayer book, in each place serving as a liturgical interlude that separates different sections of the service. It signals a change of pace, and a change in tone, as one segment of the service ends and another begins.

We are not sure who wrote the קַדִישׁ or when. It probably developed over hundreds of years. We do know that almost eight hundred years ago the קַדִישׁ came to be the prayer said by mourners. Some versions are longer (the one we are studying in this chapter, for example), and some are shorter (the one after the preliminary morning prayers and before the בָּרְכוּ). In most congregations, the קַדִישׁ is recited only in the presence of a minyan.

Do you consider it important to say the קַדִישׁ in the presence of a minyan? Explain your answer.

_____

_____

In some congregations, only the mourners and those observing *yahrzeit* — the anniversary of a loved one's death — stand as they recite the קַדִישׁ. In other congregations, everyone stands as a sign of support for the mourners and to recall those who died in the Holocaust.

What is the practice in *your* congregation?

On the eve of *Yom Hashoah*, Holocaust Memorial Day, many families light a yellow *yahrtzeit* candle. This ritual helps us keep alive the memories of those who died in the Holocaust.

At the conclusion of the קַדִּישׁ, we ask for peace — peace for the community, peace for the soul of the departed, peace for the Jewish people, peace for the world, peace for ourselves. This last line of the Mourner's קַדִּישׁ is said in Hebrew.

Perhaps the reason for the switch from Aramaic to Hebrew is this: Most of the קַדִּישׁ is directed to us, the Jewish people. It is up to us to magnify and sanctify God's name; it is up to us to make this world a place where God's presence is acknowledged and celebrated. But the last line is directed to God. We want peace in the world, it seems to say, but we cannot do it alone. For this, we need Your help, God. And while Aramaic was the language of the Jewish people of the time, Hebrew is our mother tongue. So when we seek to compose a prayer that transcends time and place, we say it in Hebrew. Thus the last line of this prayer of prayers slips back into Hebrew.

PRACTICE:

Read עֹשֶׂה שָׁלוֹם, the last line of the קַדִּישׁ.

עֹשֶׂה שָׁלוֹם   May God who makes peace

בִּמְרוֹמָיו   in the heavens,

הוּא יַעֲשֶׂה שָׁלוֹם   make peace

עָלֵינוּ וְעַל כָּל יִשְׂרָאֵל,   for us and for all Israel.

וְאִמְרוּ אָמֵן.   And say, Amen.

This is the same sentence that concludes both the עֲמִידָה and בִּרְכַּת הַמָּזוֹן (Grace after Meals). When we say עֹשֶׂה שָׁלוֹם at the end of the עֲמִידָה and the קַדִּישׁ, traditionally we take three steps backward, then bow to the left, to the right, and then forward.

21 אֵין כֵּאלֹהֵינוּ

The service has now officially come to a close; all the prayers have been said. But in a final flourish of liturgical ebullience, we add a fun, simple paean to God, one written before the ninth century CE. The tune is upbeat and lilting; the atmosphere in the congregation is light. It is an easy song to learn, an easy song to sing. The verses are identical in all five stanzas, save for the introductory words. And the first letters of the initial words of the first three stanzas, when read down as an acrostic, spell the word אָמֵן, a further indication that we are at the end.

PRACTICE:

Read אֵין כֵּאלֹהֵינוּ.

אֵין כֵּאלֹהֵינוּ,	There is none like our God,
אֵין כַּאדוֹנֵנוּ,	There is none like our Ruler,
אֵין כְּמַלְכֵּנוּ,	There is none like our Sovereign,
אֵין כְּמוֹשִׁיעֵנוּ.	There is none like our Savior.
מִי כֵאלֹהֵינוּ,	Who is like our God,
מִי כַאדוֹנֵנוּ,	Who is like our Ruler,
מִי כְמַלְכֵּנוּ,	Who is like our Sovereign,
מִי כְמוֹשִׁיעֵנוּ.	Who is like our Savior.
נוֹדֶה לֵאלֹהֵינוּ,	We will give thanks to our God,
נוֹדֶה לַאדוֹנֵנוּ,	We will give thanks to our Ruler,
נוֹדֶה לְמַלְכֵּנוּ,	We will give thanks to our Sovereign,
נוֹדֶה לְמוֹשִׁיעֵנוּ.	We will give thanks to our Savior.
בָּרוּךְ אֱלֹהֵינוּ,	Blessed is our God,
בָּרוּךְ אֲדוֹנֵנוּ,	Blessed is our Ruler,
בָּרוּךְ מַלְכֵּנוּ,	Blessed is our Sovereign,
בָּרוּךְ מוֹשִׁיעֵנוּ.	Blessed is our Savior.
אַתָּה הוּא אֱלֹהֵינוּ,	You are our God,
אַתָּה הוּא אֲדוֹנֵנוּ,	You are our Ruler,
אַתָּה הוּא מַלְכֵּנוּ,	You are our Sovereign,
אַתָּה הוּא מוֹשִׁיעֵנוּ.	You are our Savior.

PRAYER DICTIONARY

אֵין כּ
there is none like

מִי כ
who is like

נוֹדֶה ל
we will give thanks to

אַתָּה הוּא
you are

אֱלֹהֵינוּ
our God

אֲדוֹנֵנוּ
our ruler

מַלְכֵּנוּ
our sovereign

מוֹשִׁיעֵנוּ
our savior

BUILDING YOUR VOCABULARY

Study the Prayer Dictionary. Cover it, then circle the Hebrew translation for the English word or phrase on each line.

our savior	אָבִינוּ	אֱלֹהֵינוּ	מוֹשִׁיעֵנוּ
there is none like	בָּרוּךְ שׁ	אֵין כּ	אַתָּה הוּא
our ruler	אֲדוֹנֵנוּ	אֱלֹהֵינוּ	אֲבוֹתֵינוּ
our sovereign	מַלְכֵּנוּ	קִדְּשָׁנוּ	אֱלֹהֵינוּ
we will give thanks to	בָּרְכוּ אֶת	נוֹדֶה ל	לְעַמּוֹ
who is like	כִּי בָּנוּ	נוֹדֶה ל	מִי כ

Joyous music can magically bring voices — and clapping hands — together.

Prayer Building Blocks

אֵין כְּ

"there is none like"	אֵין means "there is none." כְּ is a prefix that means "like." Circle the Hebrew word and prefix meaning "there is none like" in the lines below. אֵין כֵּאלֹהֵינוּ אֵין כַּאדוֹנֵנוּ

מִי כְ

"who is like"	מִי means "who is." כְּ means "like." Circle the word and prefix meaning "who is like" in the lines below. מִי כֵאלֹהֵינוּ מִי כַאדוֹנֵנוּ

נוֹדֶה ל

"we will give thanks to"	נוֹדֶה means "we will give thanks." ל is a prefix that means _____. Circle the word and prefix meaning "we will give thanks to" in the lines below. נוֹדֶה לֵאלֹהֵינוּ נוֹדֶה לַאדוֹנֵנוּ

אַתָּה הוּא

"you are"	Circle the Hebrew words that mean "you are" in the lines below. אַתָּה הוּא אֱלֹהֵינוּ אַתָּה הוּא אֲדוֹנֵנוּ

Order of the Shabbat Morning Service

SH'MA AND ITS BLESSINGS

בָּרְכוּ

יוֹצֵר אוֹר

שְׁמַע

וְאָהַבְתָּ

מִי כָמֹכָה

AMIDAH

אָבוֹת וְאִמָּהוֹת

גְּבוּרוֹת

קְדוּשָׁה

קְדוּשַׁת הַיּוֹם

עֲבוֹדָה

הוֹדָאָה

שִׂים שָׁלוֹם

אֱלֹהַי נְצֹר

עֹשֶׂה שָׁלוֹם

TORAH SERVICE

אֵין כָּמוֹךָ

אַב הָרַחֲמִים

כִּי מִצִּיּוֹן

לְךָ יְיָ

בִּרְכוֹת הַתּוֹרָה

וְזֹאת הַתּוֹרָה

בִּרְכוֹת הַהַפְטָרָה

אַשְׁרֵי

עֵץ חַיִּים הִיא

CONCLUDING PRAYERS

עָלֵינוּ

קַדִּישׁ

אֵין כֵּאלֹהֵינוּ

מִלּוֹן